I AM a Brillia.

Volume Four

Stories of women who have gone beyond surviving to thriving in their business and life

Karen Klassen

Contributing Authors

Angela Martini

Barbara McBean

Chantal Pilon

Luanne Celine

Lisa Mundell

Deborah Janz

Sloane Hunter

Janice Kendall

Nirmala Naidoo

Nicole Stettler

I AM a Brilliant Woman Volume Four

Editors: Penn Geek and Norma Jean Maxwell

Cover Design by Design Arena

Formatting by Arty

For inquiries, please contact: Karen Klassen

www.karenklassen.ca

ISBN: 978-0-9918890-5-1

First Edition

Table of Contents

This book is dedicated to the courageous women who are awakening and reclaiming their feminine power and the men who honour them.

Introduction

Brilliance: radiating a high degree of light.

At times you may feel like you are being pulled in different directions. Your to-do list is a mile long which includes going to yoga class, pay the bills, writing that book, morning meditation, helping your kid with homework, buying a dress for your cousin's wedding, calling your girlfriend to see if she is okay and needs anything since she just broke up with her beloved, and getting the house cleaned for the dinner party tomorrow evening. You may feel exhausted, probably stressed and need to plan that much-needed vacation. You may resort to unhealthy coping strategies such flopping on your couch the weekend, eating comfort food and binge-watch reality shows. It can feel like a vicious cycle. And you wonder, how do women who have the kids, the career, and the relationship go beyond just surviving to thriving? Are they perfect women? Can a woman have it all?

I believe we can have it all. However, having it all, takes great discipline and devotion to creating a solid foundation in self-care. This means putting YOU and your health first. The journey from surviving to thriving is about loving yourself, healing your past wounds, awakening to the calling of your own soul, truly believing you deserve the best in life and that the universe always has your back. Yes, you will fail, you will fall down and sob uncontrollably, you will be judged, criticized, and seen as a fraud. This journey to *thriving* is about facing our deepest fears so we can embrace our light.

In coaching women over the last sixteen years, the one thing I have learned is that we are not meant to do this on our own. The two most common problems women have is asking for help and creating healthy boundaries. We are not meant to take this journey on our own. We need to be courageous enough to ask for help. And it is so important to become crystal clear on knowing what you will no longer tolerate in your life - what is no longer in alignment with your own values. Your journey towards thriving shows up in phases so be patient with yourself. It is the consistency that makes all the difference. Never give up on YOU and your own dreams of a better world.

This book is a collaboration of ten incredible women, each contributing one chapter based on her specialty, her expertise, her life experience, her personality and the gifts she is here to share as a source of inspiration for women.

Each woman has been on her own unique journey of challenges and setbacks to seeing beyond the obstacles that revealed a creative power to finding solutions to their problems. Every experience molded and shaped their characters guiding each to create a life on their own terms.

We all have brilliance inside waiting to be ignited. Women who truly believe in themselves can achieve whatever they desire. This does not mean it is an easy journey. It is about showing up every day to the best of your ability.

As this is the last book in the, <u>I AM a Brilliant Woman</u> series, I wanted it to reflect the heart of women who have gone beyond surviving to truly THRIVING in their career and in their life.

This book is written by women *for* women who are ready to ignite their own heart's desires. Our intention is to offer inspiration and encouragement that will ignite the reader's heart and empower her to embrace and activate her brilliance. To remind each other to say, "YES" to living a passionate and soul-inspired life. Together, we will collectively contribute to the evolution of humanity.

Together We Rise!

Karen Klassen

Founder of Women Embracing Brilliance

The Brilliant Woman Declaration

I (your name) make a heart-centered commitment that from this moment forward, I will never degrade, gossip, cut down, or say mean or spiteful words to or about another woman. She is my sister and is a reflection of who I am. I love myself way too much to speak negatively about others.

And so it is.

In Shining Our Light, We Liberate Others

By Angela Martini

"Our deepest fear is not that we are inadequate. Our deepest fear is that we are powerful beyond measure. It is our light, not our darkness that most frightens us. We ask ourselves, who am I to be brilliant, gorgeous, talented, fabulous? Actually, who are you not to be? You are a child of the universe. You're playing small does not serve the world. There is nothing enlightened about shrinking so that other people won't feel insecure around you. It's not just in some of us; it's in everyone.

And as we let our own light shine, we unconsciously give other people permission to do the same. As we are liberated from our own fear, our presence automatically liberates others."

I remember distinctly being told over and over again as a child that wanting more, wanting too much from life, would result in "bad things" happening to me. Growing up in Austria, in a small-town old wives' tales and superstitions became my reality.

Insulated by steep mountains, long cold winters, a rich history steeped in folklore and tradition, my mind was forged by my elders. It was my Oma, whom I spent most of my time with growing up, that tried to keep me safe from my lofty goals, thoughts and my need for freedom.

I have always been a dreamer; positive, happy, and unafraid to try new things. Much to my mother and my grandmother's dismay. I was the oldest child and therefore, needed to set an example for my two younger sisters.

And so, I grew up in a small town surrounded by farmland and cows, with strict rules, stereotypical gender roles, and a confusing message. You see, my father secretly wished for a boy, a male heir, even though he was blessed with three girls: Angela, Claudi, and Martina. We even had male nicknames, which we were lovingly given to us by our Papa.

The entire neighbourhood knew us by these names and I was often made fun of. When I reflect back on my childhood, I do so with many fond memories. There was love and a deep sense of belonging but there was also confusion and so many limits imposed by our circumstances.

There were also times in my childhood when felt truly like "me", really felt free when I was with my pony, Jenny. I would ride as fast as I could with my long brown hair waving in the wind. I rode through our neighbouring farmers' fields, along the river and tall grasses dreaming of a life far away from home. My imagination ran wild, like my black Shetland pony, and I knew back then that I would leave this place called "Heimat" to grow and expand and make my mark.

In my teenage years, I earned fantastic grades but as no one in my immediate family had ever attended post-secondary education, I was destined to follow in their footsteps and work as an apprentice in a shoe store.

At the age of fifteen, my parents escorted me to my very first formal dance and I fell in love for the first time. He was eighteen, tall, handsome and had been raised in Canada. A three-year romance and long-distance relationship resulted in me moving away at the tender age of eighteen.

I decided to leave it all behind, my country, my family, my sisters and all that I knew to be true. I followed my first love to Canada, to freedom and the land of opportunity. Austrians view Canada as a sort of promise land and many dream of escaping and immigrating there.

Today, I realize that I don't often allow myself to look back at the moment I left my parents and my crying sisters at the airport in Munich. In 1983 passengers of overseas flights still dressed up, and so did I. I wore a beautiful cream and beige suit, a new blouse, pantyhose, and high heel shoes. I looked back at my mother's teary eyes and it would be years until I returned back home for the very first visit. No cell phones, no internet, and an awkward and expensive phone system meant that I had to mostly communicate via letters.

I arrived in this foreign country with limited English language skills, all my belongings stuffed into two suitcases and unexpected, indescribable cultural differences. I embarked on years of growth and discovery but many nights I would cry myself to sleep suffering with unbearable homesickness and the confusion of loving the challenge all the while.

A few years later I found myself alone. The man I loved and gave up so much for, left me in debt and with no credit rating. I was devastated and once again affirmed in my belief that I just wanted too much from life.

My Austrian pride would not allow me to return home broke and broken and so I attended night school and worked two jobs to just to get by. I knew with more education I would be granted more opportunity and this determination led me to eventually graduate from University of Alberta.

Looking back now, these challenges prepared me to be open and to finding the love of my life, a career that fulfills me, and the family and life that I had imagined as a young girl.

My second husband and life companion Joe, brought new energy into my life. The son of immigrant Italian parents, he was groomed to be educated and to rise above his parents' circumstances. Luckily for me, he dreamt and still dreams, even bigger dreams than I do and encourages me to continue to grow and expand and always be in the YES energy.

Many years later, in the midst of a twin pregnancy, different careers, businesses, and a passion-filled life with opportunities for growth and learning, a new horizon appeared. I was introduced to the profession of Network Marketing. I was skeptical at first, but the product created a result that was undeniable. Today, I am so thankful I was open to changing my mind and career.

The limiting belief of "bad things" happening when I wanted more from life was abolished one small goal, set and reached, at a time.

In this business model, I finally started to eliminate the fear of success, the fear of not being good enough, and the fear of wanting more. When I chose to step into leadership in my newfound career, I knew that I had to level up, I knew I had to lead, I knew there was no more hiding. I became a student of the Network Marketing profession that is so often misunderstood.

In standing up for the profession, in getting educated and rising above all judgment, I found my strength in just helping people get better physically and supporting them on their journey. When I get lost in the service of others and get invested in helping people reach their goals, I forget all about the things that might hold me back. I let my light shine bright, I let my belief rub off and magic happens. Thousands of people have miraculously shown up and it has created a ripple effect that continues today.

The most powerful example of breaking through this story in my head was setting a record earning goal and achieving it. Best of all never worrying about me but focusing solely on creating results for others.

So, the story I was told, the story that kept me safe is no longer the story that keeps me stuck and limits my growth. Whatever story you may have been told to believe, whatever limiting belief still exists in us, we can break free of it. What a liberating feeling! And in shining our bright light we liberate others.

When I was first presented with the opportunity to share a piece of my story in this book, I was challenged with the title, as I have always thought of myself as a thriver not just a survivor. In all life's turmoil and chaos, I believed and trusted in me and my ability to see myself through any obstacle, and to grow through the struggle at hand.

I also realize that given the same circumstances people will react differently based on their upbringing and conditioning as a child. We get to choose to be the victim or the victor. By nature, I have always chosen to thrive. My mother's tales about Sunday children, which I am one of, entertains the notion that we are the "lucky" ones and that we will lead a great life.

Today, I find myself in the right place, aligned with my purpose, still in love after thirty plus years with my soul's companion, Joe, and proud to have raised incredible twin daughters that have grown up in a home and conversation that allows them to freely explore their gifts.

I am thankful for the journey, I am in gratitude for all the tears, hardships and that I have found my light that allows others to shine bright. When we realize that life happens for us and not to us, we can clearly see the brilliance in the struggle, the rise, and the growth. There are many more chapters to come and I embrace them with excitement, knowing that thriving is a conscious choice we get to make.

I AM a brilliant woman.

Three gems every woman needs to be successful and happy in their life:

1. Every woman has the right to understand that she has all that she needs inside of her, that her brilliance is unique just waiting to be applied to her true purpose in life. Give it time, listen and be open to new experiences that may reveal your true gift to the world.

2. Every woman has her own definition of what's possible and that success is to be defined by her own soul's desire and the ability to tap fully into her unique brilliance. Often this unique innate gift can be found and amplified in service to others. The definition of success is fluid and will change over time, be kind with yourself and be aware of the sideward glance and comparison to others.

3. Every woman has the choice and right to be happy daily, in the present moment, embracing life and growth in her own brilliant way.

Happy is a state of mind, a moment, fleeting and can be discovered in the nooks and crannies of life. When we become aware and observant of all the beauty around us – happiness is but a state of being.

About Angela

Angela Martini immigrated to Canada from Austria in her late teens with two suitcases and a dream. She is the mother of identical twins and is married to the love of her life Joe.

She is a passionate entrepreneur, with a diverse background in health and wellness.

In her late 40's, Angela was introduced to network marketing following an incredible product experience, that took her on a journey to the fitness stage.

Angela fell in love with the culture and leadership of her partner company, built a team of thousands and today as a top income earner, prides herself on the ability to combine her love for people, team building and creating both health and wealth results.

Her unique ability to see brilliance in others has made her a mentor to many, a trusted source for women on transformational health journeys and an advocate for women rising.

Angela can be contacted at angela@angelaamartini.com

I AM a brilliant woman because I see brilliance in others before they see it in themselves.

– Angela Martini

I AM a Brilliant Woman

The Road Was Not Paved with Golden Bricks

By Barbara McBean

"I believe that every person has a path and a journey they are on in this life. Unlimited potential is something every woman (and man) has inside of them. But unlimited potential does not always equal unlimited happiness and success. The key to finding your highest purpose takes a lot of guts, hard work and the ability to never give up or give in!"

The story of my personal road to success was certainly not paved with golden bricks. There have been a lot of obstacles, challenges, and certainly some crazy adventures along the way. I was born into a fairly modestly normal, middle-income family. Until the age of seven years old, life was pretty much as awesome as any child could hope for. Then, like so many families... we experienced a complete implosion of all things good. My parents went through a separation and ultimately divorced. But this was no mild separation. In truth, it was an all-out war and my sister and I were put in the middle of the most intense, hateful energy between the two people we loved and needed the most in our lives at that time. Finally, when the dust settled and all the carnage was had… we were four very broken human beings each in our own ways. What came next for my Mother, my sister and I were some very dark years filled with poverty, loss, many struggles, and a lot of painful situations.

I knew from a very young age that I did not want to struggle with the basics of just subsistence living. I watched my Mom have to budget constantly just to get by and never really being able to dream about adventure or better yet changing the world. We lived to survive. So definitely the first motivation for my work ethic was the ability to move beyond poverty.

I was incredibly creative and loved the arts when I was a child. I also loved the world of glamour and fashion! I would look at the magazines for hours and dream of becoming one of the elegant women that graced their pages. I certainly tried out for model searches and all of the silly things young girls do in their teen years. But I was still just an awkward puffy-haired blonde girl from the wrong side of town. I did have one secret weapon… and that was my intelligence. I was always very quiet and shy but I loved to study the world and watch and listen to everything around me. And so, day-by-day, week-by-week, I learned how to excel at the art of make-up and styling myself. You would not have believed the outfits I could create straight off the racks of Value Village. Man! I would walk into school looking like a million bucks with the most unique outfits anyone had ever seen!

I also loved to work! To me, work meant hope for a better life and self-pride. I was pretty young for my very first job. At ten years old I would help sell fruit at the farmer markets. I understood how to interact with the customers and I loved giving them an excellent shopping experience! And I was grateful for the jingle in my pocket after a hard day's work! Money is not always about greed. Money is the currency of diligent hard work. Money allows us to create happy and safe surroundings, put food on the table and make way for the fun adventures that money will often lead to.

Throughout the years I was honoured to work at many jobs, and they all taught me something new and very valuable. From working on sculptured masterpieces with Artistic Ceilings by TD in the evenings while I was in high school, to Subway, Little Caesar's Pizza, waitressing at many local diners, cleaning houses, retail sales, dog walking… you name it I did it and usually had 2-3 jobs all the time.

Although I did attend university for several years and also SAIT for oil and gas administration, my passion always came back to art and beauty. I do believe that was how brands like Eternal Beauty Institutes, Vidalash, DigitexPro, Plasmalift and many more of my companies were born; with the help of all my previous experiences and hard work combined with a Dream and a purpose to create something different.

It took years to believe in the woman I was and the ability in my own skills to take a leap of faith. I put every ounce of my being into what was inside my head and then allowed my heart to lead me there.

There is no doubt in life we will all face challenges. The beauty and curse of life is that we really do not know what the future holds. We can only try to plan accordingly and do our best. I know my heart has always been in the right place but when in business you need to take risks and that is what it's all about. You will experience judgment, competition and some really tough problems. So, cultivating problem-solving skills is a must.

Overcoming Challenges

I think the first and most difficult challenge I had to overcome was certainly my own battle with mental illness. I don't believe that I was born with a mental illness just a very sensitive disposition and delicate brain chemistry. Anxiety has always been a very frustrating part of my existence. I truly wish I did not have to battle it daily. In business, there are a lot of high-pressure and super stressful things that crop up daily. I have learned to manage my stress with diet, exercise and good rest. I think sleep is one of the most crucial factors for a healthy brain. One doctor described it to me so well and it has always stuck with me. "When you sleep your brain is essentially in it's wash cycle. It recalibrates everything from your daily reality and rebalances you". I liked that and I have always used sleep as a tool to hit the reset button on my brain. I even have a daybed in my office and if I must, I sleep in the middle of the day even for thirty minutes just to put myself into a calmer state of mind to tackle the obstacles ahead!

The second most difficult challenge I had to overcome in my life was my own common law separation. I had worked very hard in my youth and at seventeen years old I managed to buy my first home. Through my early 20's I built my first business; a tanning salon chain in my home town with two locations. I had beautiful in-laws that I loved to pieces and it just seemed like I was going to have a beautiful life. I even competed for the Miss Universe competition! Then I was blind-sided and everything fell apart all around me. My fiancé was battling his own inner demons which my young mind and lack of experience did not understand. He had become addicted to crack cocaine. I didn't even really know what was going on for probably two years - as I was so dedicated to my school, my jobs and just getting ahead. But when things started to unravel oh boy… it was like a real-life episode of "Intervention". I won't get into the horrible details as that would really be a book all in itself. It was the most terrifying, dangerous, and difficult time for me and probably a big reason I am so humble and hardworking still to this day. In a time when my ego and self-confidence was being challenged, everything came crashing down. I lost my house, which I was so proud of. You can't really understand how it breaks one's heart to lose your home like that… especially considering growing up all I wanted was one stable place to call home. I had finally made it for myself! I'd spent two years to renovate inside and out, and then due to someone's addiction, it was all gone. Everything, once again, fell into pieces around me. It was like being seven years old all over again. I lost my first love, I lost his family, I lost my home, I lost my businesses. I lost everything I had worked so hard for in my teens. Worse yet, I had to declare bankruptcy and none of it was even my doing! I was too young to understand what was really going on and by the time I had, it was too late.

But there was a silver lining … I learned to be strong. Even in the face of extremely hard choices, I could find happiness in simple things like my own safety and my own good decisions. I also realized that people can make very bad decisions. Though they were not my bad decisions, I had a bird's eye view of how someone can literally throw their life away by going down the wrong path. That experience built compassion inside me but also made me streetwise which I think especially in business has come to serve me in my later years.

The third most difficult challenge I have faced in my life thus far was building the Eternal Beauty Institute. As with any business, there are no road maps of "How to build your own post-secondary school". So, this crazy beast of a business has continued to throw me curve balls, challenges and really a lot of daily stress. But what I am beginning to understand is that I too am learning. I have a spirit for constant improvement, innovation and the intention to help women, young and old, be successful in business. And I truly believe in my core that I am the right woman for the job. It's a special feeling when you are certain you actually know the path to success.

I think each and every woman (and man) needs to realize life is full of twists and turns. There will be pain and there will be pleasure. Your heart will break wide open and you will soar with the eagles. There will always be extremely tough days, weeks, months and even years. But the key is to not give up. We all make mistakes; that is how we grow. But take those mistakes and make a better version of yourself. Do not give in to laziness, negativity or jealousy. Focus on yourself and your own goals. If you try to compare yourself to the

Kim Kardashian's of the world you will be frustrated because you didn't come from the same place, or have the same circumstances. Compare yourself to the person you were yesterday, who you are becoming today and who you want to be in the future. That should be your focus and you will find peace, I promise, in that.

When it comes to life and the wisdom of how to live it well and also how to ensure that one's life has meaning; I believe there are a few key elements. So, my words of wisdom to all the women out there are as follows…

Dream Big!

Dreams and the creative force behind them are really the basis of all success in life. Without a vision for the future, really what is the point?

As women throughout history our ability to dream has been dampened by our former position as persons in society, and in general. We are only now, in the 21st Century, beginning to remember how to dream big! But to have an idea is not enough. You need to be deeply invested in the process of building. Building truly means a lot of hard work and challenges. And I think this is one of the most important factors people these days miss. They assume a dream, or a goal will just unfold magically like in a two-hour Hollywood movie. Life, thank God, is longer than that and therefore building our dreams is not so seamless. To make your mark you must be ready for a lot of hard work. You also have to anticipate opposition and usually, the opposition will come from people that have not yet figured out their own dream or path. But fear not as while you shine your light on your journey and ultimate destination you will by way of energetic osmosis inspire so many others.

Take Care of Yourself

Another piece of wisdom I will share with you that I think is so important to happiness is to truly take care of yourself. This is not to be confused with an inflated ego or selfishness. Taking care of yourself does not mean to take advantage of others. What it means is do not make yourself a martyr. Martyrdom is really a foolish idea; I don't believe you inspire anyone by suffering on purpose. Certainly, in life, there will be pain and there will be difficult situations but intentionally putting ourselves in harm's way makes no sense. I feel that many women often justify being badly treated for reasons of the "greater good". Whether that be for her children, or her husband or the world at large. As a woman and a human being, you DO deserve to be happy. And other's happiness should not always come first. It is ok to ask your husband to help with the kids or make dinner. It is ok to say… today I am tired and I need some space. You need to fill your cup before the brilliance will shine. You also have to have a fighting spirit growing inside you. You have to learn to fight for what is right in this world. You need to fight for your own happiness. You need to fight for the happiness and prosperity of your family. As a global community, we need to have the courage to fight together for a better tomorrow. And that means you need to take care of you so that you can be an active part of our human story.

Accept What You Cannot Change

Lastly, learn to accept the things that you cannot change. Some of us were born disabled. Some of us were born into poverty while some struggle with illness or lack certain skills or aptitudes in life. Accept the things you cannot change and find ways to work within what you can handle. And let go of guilt and shame. I myself have terrible vertigo which causes anxiety about a lot of height related activities. It also gets worse the more stress I am under. I used to get down on myself and beat myself up constantly about not being perfect; or "like everyone else" … but what does that even mean? None of us are the same and we all come with a very special set of gifts and talents. So, I might not be the best rock climber in the group but I can certainly build great organizations! I shine in other ways I just need to be on the ground floor to do it. The same goes for the way we look! As women, one of the most frustrating aspects of trying to make it in this world is our constant battle with an exterior image. True beauty is in a smile and in happiness and confidence. We are all beautiful when we are at our best! So, remember to see your own gorgeous light and in that, you will not feel small or less than! You will begin to see the beauty all around you. But remember the force of beauty comes from our hearts and emanates outward magnetically interacting with the world around us!

I cannot promise all days will be easy, I cannot promise every moment will be bliss… but what I can promise is that if you live each day on purpose, that when you reach your final destination it will truly be a life worth living!

About Barbara

Barbara is the Founder & President of Eternal Beauty International and many global technology companies & beauty lines. With over twenty years of medical spa experience & ownership.

At the age of twenty, Barbara created the tanning franchise Baja Suntan Studios in Calgary, Alberta. In 2005, she competed in the prestigious Miss Universe Pageant while attending University of British Columbia. She later relocated back to Alberta to finish her studies in psychology at the University of Calgary.

Eternal Beauty was founded on the principles that education should be accessible for everyone who has the spirit to learn & grow! This passion for creating excellence is the foundation of the Eternal Beauty Group and Satellite Technology Companies & beauty brands.

To connect with Barbara visit eternalbeautyinstitute.com or www.plasmalift.ca

I AM a brilliant woman because I devote my purpose and my energy into creating, guiding and growth.

– Barbara McBean

I AM a Brilliant Woman

For the Love of Beautiful Shoes

By Chantal Pilon

No one said it would be easy to start up a shoe brand... and I am here to say it is not... I have love and support from my friends and family as well as my amazing customers who know how much love I put into my brand.

How did I know I wanted to be a shoe designer? I didn't! When I finished high school all I wanted to do was something different than everyone else. I wanted to be creative. My mother said it would be hard to make a living in the art world so from the age of fifteen I started working for my grandfather in his shoe shop. For many years, I worked three jobs at a time, both in the fashion and restaurant industries.

At one of the wholesale shoe trade shows in Las Vegas, I accompanied my mother as one of the footwear buyers for our shops. I had the pleasure to be introduced to a well-known Canadian shoe designer from Vancouver, John Fluevog, and was instantly inspired by his story. I thought to myself, "I would *love* to be a shoe designer." I loved shoes, selling and being creative. We had already been working with a few brands where we could change a few details and this was my favourite thing to do. John told me of the schools in London and Italy to research. Immediately, I looked it up and it was as if a light went on in my head.

I needed to do this! How scary! I had never left Canada or the USA! The school I found was <u>Cordwainer's</u>, a prestigious footwear college in London. Jimmy Choo and Patrick Cox, among many other high profile designers, went to this college (now known as London College of Fashion). That was it! Revelation! I was going to do it and nothing was stopping me. My mom was fully on board as she could see the light switched on in me.

I studied for two years and I felt alive, really alive! I couldn't believe I left Canada and my family but it felt so right. All the ideas and excitement in my head were now going to come to life. During my two years of study, I made shoes by hand and built sole units in my small dorm room like a mad scientist. I stayed up late every night drawing and creating all my projects with fervor. Plus, I was living in London!

After two years, I finished the most amazing time in college and decided to go back to Canada and find a design job. It was not so easy as I thought. I ended up finding a job at Clarks in Somerset UK, where I travelled to China, Brazil, all of Europe and USA looking for inspiration, working with factories developing and preparing for production. I spent a very successful 4 1/2 years at Clarks. I went from a junior to a senior designer in my time there. I had many top ten styles and developed a sub-line, which was phenomenal. Then I was headhunted to work for Kenneth Cole in New York. Kenneth moved my entire life to New York City. This was a huge change for me from a small village in the UK. Now, I was surrounded by the concrete jungle. I worked at Kenneth Cole (KCP) for five years - what a wonderfully inspiring man. A talented shoe designer and philanthropist; I owe many of my work ethics to him.

What an amazing job, and even more important, being part of another person's dream. I travelled on his private jet visiting European cities in search of inspiration, development planning and working closely with him for the final collections. I had a team of young designers and I set the work and planning for each season. I had to present the line with my team to our sales team, Nordstrom's and other big department stores. Kenneth was always a warm-hearted employer and was very supportive of my work.

The only issue after five years was that I had a British husband and a new-born son and I had to rethink my career. My husband could not work in the USA and it was driving him crazy. So, we up and left to come back to the UK where I free-lanced for many companies. The freedom was a nice change, plus I had quality time with my new little family.

One day, I was approached by a Canadian company to start a wholesale brand. I was starting to be known for my style. We started in Portugal as the quality is amazing and the factories have more flexibility. The shoe group wanted low prices and basic product. I thought, "Isn't there enough of this mass production, same old boring mediocre quality footwear out there?" I said to myself, "Where has all the identity of one's self gone? Is everyone turning into sheep??" I was never a sheep.

I was never an ordinary child. When I stood in line up at school, I felt my physical body was in the line up but my mind was not. I knew I did not want to be an ordinary person… but not sure why. I wasn't the "brains" or the popular kid in school. I didn't care about those things. I didn't follow anyone. I was the kid that was bullied... for being unique and having a mother who was divorced (not as common in those days). I always was a maker of my own fashion and hairstyles when I was young and was very inquisitive… a busy brain.

Today, I look at my eldest son Jagger and I see him outside the line. It makes me smile. I think he is a lot smarter and more popular than what I ever was at his age. I do feel his inner torment, as it is not easy for him to put his finger on why he is standing outside the line... nor can I... but he belongs there, as it is the right place for him. Like me, he needs to be busy, to create what pops into his head and create it with whatever tools he can find. It is like a release. I believe; this is how all creative minds feel at some point.

How did I become the woman I am today? I was bullied in school, had average grades and had few friends. I always had at least one good friend to support me and love me for who I was. I also think it was a lot to do with fate and faith.... and a lot of support.

One day my husband said, "Why don't you start your own line?" Hmmm… I knew this would be the biggest challenge of my life. I had found some lovely factories and already built strong relationships and I was very particular how a product had to be designed to mean something to the consumer. Wow! There it was again! That light… and it went off in my head and knew I needed to do it.

In early 2012, I began to develop the Chanii B brand in Portugal. The name comes from (my childhood nickname Chanii and the B stands for to B… Inspired… B… Admired. B… Individual. This is what I was going to create.

The product speaks for itself with all leather lining, comfortable fitting and with an edgy, artsy, rocker edge, that appeals to the woman who desires to make a statement and an entrance with her shoes and feel amazing all day and night.

I wanted my brand to stand-alone from all this mass-marketing where there is no love just cheap throwaway product. I wanted to reach into my grandfather's roots and beliefs. He used to say, "You can tell a lot about a person by the shoes they wear."

My grandfather was a Coldstream Guard in England. After the war, he went to work with Bata shoes. Back then, shoes were made with great quality and pride behind the workmanship. Plus, the service in the stores were carving out a way for future stores - to care about their customers. After many successful years opening shops for Bata in England, the Bahamas and Canada, he decided to open his own shoe company which he called, Checkmate Shoes (still based in Calgary). He wanted to bring a higher quality of footwear to his shops and provide exceptional service. Today, my mother paves the way as the owner of Checkmate and Shoe Muse bringing comfortable high-end shoes and accessories to fashionistas and women who love quality and comfort.

My husband and I were blessed with another son, Phoenix. Then halfway into 2012, I opened my first flagship shop in Bath, in the UK which was supposed to be a pop-up shop. Now seven years later the brand is taking off. I cultivated a strong customer base. I have people from all over the world coming to my shop in Bath and they are always looking forward to my new creations. Chanii B is known for their array of colour and individuality using quality leathers and material, with a fuchsia leather lining. Always comfortable and timeless.

I am blessed with all of the love of a supportive family and friends, as I could not have reached this dream without them. It is not my nature to ask for help. However, over the years I have learned we all need to have our angels on earth who believe in us and to be a part of our dreams.

The brand is obsessively loved by many. I follow my vision and dream of unique and beautifully crafted women's shoes… and they need to be comfortable … and they are! I tell my customers that each shoe I design from beginning to end has a different story before they are on a customer's foot. Some styles I have had to fight to get the patterns correct as I do not accept the idea, "it can't be done." I am stubborn and I will find a way! And we do, most of the time. It's great to be challenged and the reward is that my styles are loved by many.

I have designed for ladies going to tea at the Queen's gardens, for the women attending the races at Ascot, for celebrities on TV in Canada plus for many brides who wish to walk down the aisle in a comfortable beautiful pair of Chanii B's. They are also able to dance the night away without having to take them off and still be comfortable.

Today, it is still a woman in a man's world. First of all, women are not taken seriously, I remember a work trip I took at the beginning of my work related traveling and someone said to me, "How can you be here making shoes when you have young children at home?" That was a painful question. I replied, "My husband is at home with the children and this is my job, which I love!" Strong role models are important as they need to have great mentors in their life. Men have more freedom to build their business relationships (like in many other industries) by taking out extra family time with golfing, fishing and sports with work colleagues. We women do not fit into this way of working. We usually have children to attend to at the end of a busy day and are still expected to be with our families and still fit the old fashioned mold. We are all very proud to be able to juggle the family and work-life in pursuit of our dreams. Women like me take different approaches to business, such as networking and word of mouth.

Now in the brands seventh year, the most challenging thing for me is figure out how to get the brand out in the market when

I am already so busy with one season in hand where I work in the shop plus I am selling to the wholesalers for the next season. Then immediately, I am designing and developing the next season twelve months in advance. On top of that I am then having to purchase leathers and mold's ahead of the work. An endless cycle. Oh but I love it!

As there is only one of me, I will need a bigger team with the knowledge and skills to grow the brand. I will also need to juggle my time with my family life and my retail shop. To achieve this next growth step I will need to look for professional guidance and investors.

I have funded this brand from the beginning through hard work, being the designer, developer, and the salesperson in my shop (when I am there). Plus, I take on contracts to help design and rebuild brands to have an identity. This is what I do best. But I still remember I have two amazing children and a husband that I love to spend quality time with. And all the while, next season's inspiration is bubbling inside me to create more amazing well-made Chanii B's!

Everyone says to me I need to get my shoes on celebrities. However, they want to be paid to wear them and then there is still no guarantee they will endorse your brand. I find this frustrating as I am a one-woman band and, they say it takes a village to be successful. But that doesn't stop me! I currently hire apprentices to teach my trade to and help me with the amount of work I have. I love teaching my passion and knowing I am inspiring young students to grow and learn great business skills.

My four keys of wisdom for all women wishing to pursue their dreams are.

Get lots of support emotionally and believe in yourself

Surround yourself with positive passionate people to empower your dreams and help pick you up when you are down. You need them to remind you why and what brought you to this road to starting your dream.

Be thankful for everything

Be thankful for everything in this world and the life you have every day. Remember to soak in the beauty of our world ... do more than stop and smell the roses. Every day has stress and challenges. Have a good scream if needed to release some stress then center yourself for a few minutes each day and realize how lucky you are to be alive.

Challenge yourself

Challenge yourself by making your goals reachable but hard enough to keep that spark alive in you to grab it, achieve it and want for more. Never give up! Realize you are paving the road of your dream. When you are following your dreams - you are going to trip along the way. That's part of life as we are not perfect and there is no manual. Perseverance! Perseverance! Perseverance!

Be an exceptional role model for your children.

I have a lot of guilt, especially when I have to travel for work and be away from my children. It's the hardest part of my career. I remind myself that it shows my children work ethics and determination. I include them in my design work and when new samples I have completed come in they are excited about my creations. They even have an opinion!

About Chantal

Canadian born with three generations in the shoe business and with a love for fashion Chantal gave up everything in Canada to study and work in the UK and NY and to follow her dream. After many years designing for companies, and with all the moral support from her mother and family, Chantal developed Chanii B.

From the beginning, Chanii B has been driven from all of Chantal's passion for something different and beautiful. All Chanii B's are made in Portugal in small factories. They are made with luxury leathers and details and are full of color and comfortable for all-day wear. Bespoke orders are a favourite of Chantal's as she loves making extra special, one of kind shoes and bags for that special day. Chantal sells Chanii B in Bath UK at her flagship shop plus boutiques in Canada and USA. Chanii B customers are obsessed with the brand now seven years old and love all the amazing creations Chantal develops. It's all for the love of beautiful shoes! Find your perfect pair or pairs of Chanii B's and you will be asked, "Where did you get these shoes?"

I wish to dedicate this to my mom who is my fearless hero, mentor and best friend. I couldn't have dreamed to do this without her endless love and belief in me.

To connect with Chantal visit chaniib.com or chaniibshoes.com

I AM a brilliant woman because my creations and passion can bring happiness and strength to any woman by wearing Chanii B.

– Chantal Pilon

I AM a Brilliant Woman

The Art of Precious Scars

By Luanne Celine

When people ask me to describe my metamorphosis, I say the first thing that comes to mind: "It felt like I was being skinned alive".

Though the description may have shock value and may evoke disturbing imagery, it is apt. It was an extremely painful time, but one which spoke truth to my identity. I was forced to shed my adapted skin and embrace vulnerability. I was forced to think about thinking about feeling again. I'll explain.

It was 2015 and, from the outside, my life probably looked pretty good to most (I was a master of smoke and mirrors). I had been working as a lawyer at the same reputable firm since landing the position after law school.

Lawyer by day and dance instructor by night, I was operating dance studios in two cities with successful students. I had a nice house with a view, a decent car and I travelled often. I was also married without children (the only dependent other than my husband was a small dog), I had enough money to buy whatever pair of designer shoes I wanted that month. I had fake nails, fake hair, and false eyelashes. At that time, I would not have described myself as unhappy, even though I would later learn that I had buried a lot of my personality quirks and personal desires in under an ersatz image of success and perfection.

Through dance, I had the opportunity to travel to countries around the world coaching brilliant dancers. I called it wanderlust. I am now told that those around me called it escapism and, in hindsight, I guess a lot of it was. But without illusion, there is no motivation. Having assiduously cast myself as a *prima donna* in a playhouse idyll of perfection and success, I couldn't quite learn the lines and grew increasingly defiant of the role. Yet, too stubborn to admit defeat, I travelled to become anonymous—to recreate myself. I lived in fleeting moments.

As my 30th birthday approached, I planned a big party in Las Vegas. I envisioned this milestone to be some grand turning point where I would suddenly morph into a happy, successful, thriving new me. I had drawn a line in the sand: this would be the decade where I would become a partner at my firm, buy a luxury vehicle and build a bigger house. Real-life could not have been more diametrically opposed.

Soon after my return from the birthday celebrations, it became apparent that the loss of my marriage was going to be the first in a series of blows to my perfect identity.

It wasn't that he was a horrible man, but we had very little in common in terms of shared values, goals and aspirations. He had no interest in my work and grew tired of the extra commitment of the dance school. I had no interest in his hobbies and did not try to take an interest. We were roommates whose contempt for one another insidiously grew. And contempt is the pasture upon which feeds resentment.

I could have tried to make it work, but that was what was written for my perfect character, my contempt for whom had now become untenable.

Then things went completely off-script. I learned that my father was having some medical testing done, which eventually revealed what would become an aggressive form of stomach cancer. By April 2015, he was having multiple surgeries and continuous rounds of chemotherapy, and this would continue on for two years. I slowly lost control and went into crisis mode. I did what many do, and grasped at anything that gave me a sense of control.

To add to the chaos, I came to the stark realization that I was at a crossroads in my career and I had to make some tough decisions— and fast. The notion of leaving relative comfort and starting at a new firm loomed large as a potentially fatal identity blow. Would I somehow be admitting that I had failed to embrace my career? But was it really *my* failure? To be unhappy at work, working on files that did not interest me? I yearned to practise exclusively in intellectual property law, but there was little support at my then firm for this development. Mentorship opportunities were limited and fraught. Indeed, I was told directly by one woman that the reason she did not want to work with me was because of the way I looked. By contrast, I learned that that was precisely why some males *wanted* to work with me. (A male partner made such a statement directly to me on a night of heavy drinking.)

It became difficult to differentiate whether it was my ability or my looks that qualified me at this firm, and this had a perverse way of further eroding my self-confidence. Work is a sensitive topic for me—always has been. I've always had an inferiority complex, which manifested in the belief that I was ill-suited or not smart enough for the law. Generally speaking, I have often felt different than most other lawyers, and certainly did not have the same silver spoon upbringing as most of my contemporaries. This great chink in my armour, in retrospect, left me vulnerable to predation at the hands of entitled men or, at times, That cherite-type women.

Instinctively, I knew that in order to have a fulfilling career, I had to either move out east to practice intellectual property law or I had to go with a national firm. I chose the latter and, with a mix of poignancy and relief, tendered my resignation in June of 2016.

Consumed by the fear of upsetting my family during the time of my father's health crisis and clinging desperately to the once-motivating illusion of perfection, I told no one about my moribund marriage nor my professional move. I fancied myself quite the actor; but I failed to account for an intuitive friend and mentor who had known me since my childhood. There's no fooling her. She was the woman who helped me start my first business, showed me the joys of travelling abroad, educated me on the delicacies of Indian food and, perhaps most importantly, tutored me in the ways of righteousness and in the importance of having two eyebrows as opposed to one. This woman had experienced a similar death and I admired how she reinvented herself, each time stronger than the last. This phoenix made me listen to my instinct. Mired in uncertainty but spurred by possibility, I did just that.

Strange things began to happen. I started to *feel* more intensely. I would go on long walks and turn to poetry and music to settle the inferno within. I actively and outwardly practiced gratitude and modesty. I began to admit weakness and defeat— perhaps the result of intense stress from being in crisis for so long. But I felt a calming strength begin to build within. I knew instinctively that things were about to get very difficult. This both terrified and excited me.

As I navigated this tense time, I chanced upon someone who changed my life forever. As I was contemplating a work change, a notice came that a new lawyer would be starting at the firm. His name was familiar, but aside from that, I knew nothing more about the candidate. I reached out to a friend (actually a guy who I had had a bit of a fling with who, ironically turned out to have been this guy's best friend in law school) to inquire. I put two and two together, I realized he was the son of a lovely couple whom I often got to see at each of the Christmas parties at my former firm (his father is a former partner, now a federal judge, and I always had a natural draw to his witty, intelligent mother).

One sunny afternoon in April 2016, I was feeling overwhelmed with the rate of change in my life. I sent out an email to my colleagues asking if anyone wanted to go for coffee. Some responded, but when it came down to action, the only person who joined was this new colleague. We were both troubled. With heavy hearts for different reasons, we walked, grabbed an espresso and then sat on a red steel bench. This guy was absolute chaos. But he made the chaos in my heart settle flat. Inexplicably, soon we would reveal to each other our weaknesses and the messy parts of our lives that made us who we were. He would teach me to take a compliment and I would teach him to not feel ashamed for what he perceived to be failures.

I spent that summer feeling and loving. I also got to spend more time with my family as we worked through my father's illness. I was able to quietly observe my mother and father together and grew to understand what deep and true love looked like (and that I had yet to experience it). I spent that summer talking about and enjoying music, literature, and art. I was out evenings with new friends who became family. I learned the guitar and began playing the piano again. Rather than feeling ashamed for the time commitment it took, I reengaged with my love for dance. Suddenly everything shifted from gray scale to colour. So began the revivification of the self!

As the end of summer drew near, instinctively, I knew that I had some final work to do. I planned a trip to Mexico because shit was about to get real. Escapism, right? Or, a time of mental preparation for the greatest loss of all. For the first time since my 30th birthday, I was able to sit back and try (impossibly) to figure out where it all went wrong, where I was at, and what was next. For the first time since the unravelling, I allowed myself to mourn and I allowed myself to let go of the idea of what my life was "supposed" to look like. Despite the trouble, I had finally succeeded in burning my script.

Returning home, things were not easy; but I had done some important grief work. My best friend and I wept after a dance workshop and held each other, knowing that although life was really tough at this time, it was not yet at its worse. Dad would decline more rapidly, but I focussed on my time with him and loving him the best way I could. Following this modicum of personal growth, I finally publicly told people about the ended marriage. While it fell on deaf ears for some, my father understood. One of his last conversations with me was "Lu will do what Lu will do". He knew that, instinctively, I knew what I wanted and needed out of life and that I would go after it. It was almost like he gave me final permission to divorce myself from everything and anything that was no longer serving me.

My father died on November 25, 2016. I was at a Christmas party when I got the news. I rushed to the palliative care unit. I burst into the room in a floor-length red dress in time to hold my father's hand one last time and tell him how much I love him. He died moments later. He had been waiting for me.

Following my father's death, there was a great deal of mourning, but also a sense of liberation and growth. That loss (and all the other losses) forced me to acknowledge that life is not perfect. It forced me to accept that "perfection", especially of the self, is elusive at best, and perhaps impossible. It spurred me to live authentically instead of trying to be the girl in the play. It also caused me to identify and choke off parasitic relationships. I would no longer play host to the predation of others. I finally felt "permitted" to grow and thrive. I was now at liberty to tap into and follow my instinct.

I am now working in a job where I get to practise intellectual property law. The man from the red bench—we're married now. He is most difficult, for the right therapist, a *magnum* opus. But, he listens to me. He encourages me and he partners me. He celebrates my strengths, works with me on my weaknesses and challenges me. He supports me in living a life that is authentic to me. We accept and celebrate that I was never meant for the suburbs or surfing Pinterest. I don't like pumpkin spice lattes. I don't want to share recipes and I don't want to eat dinner by 6 pm each night. I am now running two dance schools in sister cities and view this business as an opportunity rather than an obligation. I no longer seek an opportunity to escape from my life, because perhaps for the first time in my adult years, I am home.

As I reflect on the loss and where I am now, I realize that change can be tough. It may even feel like you are being skinned alive. It may feel like your image of perfection has been shattered into a million pieces. But, sometimes, that is precisely what you need. For me, with all the pain came wonderful lessons and a few regulations:

1. **Divorce yourself from anything that does not allow you to grow:** you alone are in charge of your life and in order to grow, it is necessary to eliminate poison from your life.

2. **There is no perfect life**: embrace the asymmetry and unpredictability in ourselves and in life.

3. **Be insistent on your tempo and do not lose your instinct**: even in the toughest times, there will be an aperture. You must be alive to that possibility.

I will never forget 2015. I was left so broken, bereft and agitated that I was forced to dig out of all the shame and the disappointment of not living up to some identity of perfection that I had created in my mind. All of that loss and grit is part of me as I move forward. I especially love these parts of me because of what they produced. The loss created a final pressure of sorts that pressed so hard into the unsettled parts of my life, that when the gruelling time was over, I emerged, newly forged.

As I reflect on this, the Japanese art of Kintsugi comes to mind and, in closing, I will leave the reader with this note:

When a vase breaks into a thousand pieces, we often throw the pieces away regretfully. But there is an alternative. Kintsugi mends the broken pieces together with lacquer resin laced with gold and, instead of restoring the item back to its initial state, the technique actually highlights and reveres the scarred design and, ironically, the vase becomes stronger.

About Luanne

Luanne was born and raised in Saskatchewan. From a young age, Luanne had a keen interest in business and began running her own business at the age of twenty-one where, under mentorship, she received her formal Irish dance accreditation and began running a dance studio in Saskatoon. She later opened a dance studio in Regina and continues to teach classes and operate dance studios in both cities, fostering creativity in dance, fitness, and other art forms.

While growing her business, Luanne attended the University of Saskatchewan College of Arts and Science and subsequently, the College of Law. Luanne has been practising law since completing her law degree in 2010. Her practice focusses on intellectual property information technology law, where she advises clients on copyright, trademarks, domain name protection, and disputes, privacy, licensing and commercialization strategies, and other intellectual property transactions. Luanne's practice also focusses on corporate law and governance and commercial law, ranging from start-ups and small businesses to multinational public companies.

Luanne and her partner Michael reside in Saskatoon. In their spare time away from the office, they love to travel, especially to Italy, and enjoy tasting and writing about the wines they find in their travels.

I AM a brilliant woman as I learned to love all parts of myself.

– Luanne Celine

I AM a Brilliant Woman

What Happened To Me Happened For Me

By Lisa Mundell

I remember my first gift of mentorship…

I was twenty and I had just moved from Kelowna to Vancouver. I had landed a good job with Montreal Trust (later to be Scotia Bank) I had built great rapport with one of my clients, his name was Mr. Alberta Zion. Albert reminded me of my grandfather; he was kind, smart and always had a funny story for me when he came in to do his weekly banking.

Albert's family had started Acme Towel and Linen Supply, just like on Bugs Bunny! I had learned in one of the many stories he told me over the years we were working together, that his parents had sold their very large USA based company to man named Bugsy Segal and that was how money laundering had begun and he had shown me many pictures backing up this tale…

Over the course of the next six months, Albert would teach me about money exchange and how to make a good return. In exchange, I would give him the stock tips passed on to me by other clients. Alberta was always excited to share his knowledge and I was always eager to learn.

One afternoon on his usual Wednesday trip to the bank, Alberta sat at my desk and told me how his last stock tip did, and that he had made over 100K in profit. I was so very excited for him. Then he looked at me and asked if I would come and work for him full time. I was shocked and just not sure what to say. A few days later Albert and I went to lunch. That was the day my path changed!!

Albert asked me what I wanted to do when I grew up and if I wanted to earn a good living? What kind of imprint did I want to leave on the world? At the age of twenty, I had no idea what this meant to me. I can't even remember what we talked about next. I remember saying that there was a Chanel suite that I wanted to own one day… really that is the imprint I wanted to leave on the world…sigh, oh to be twenty again.

The Monday after our lunch I gave my two weeks notice. I remember being so scared and yet so excited at the same time. That's when I started down this new path and I am so grateful for being twenty and not having limiting beliefs. I had just started my first six-figure job!

Alberta believed in what he would call "trial by fire learning" and to this day it still makes me smile. I use it often with my new trainees and colleagues and this my friend, you can't learn from a book. As we didn't have a formal office we would meet at the White Spot every day for breakfast and brief what the day ahead looked like.

On day one, we drove around most of the day looking at the building he owned and the ones he decided not to buy. He gave great detail as to the reason why he bought certain buildings both from the standpoint of the building itself and all of the financials behind it. Alberta took his time pointing out all of the great things about each building… you know, the things that most people don't really notice in the details that the Architect put into each building. Nearing the end of the day he took me to two more buildings. Albert asked me what I saw in each building and to explain to him what I saw, each detail big and small. He reminded me that I needed to feel each building and I need to listen to what it was saying back to me. I didn't really understand what he meant by that, but I told him what I saw and how I felt about them.

Day two; was just like a movie for me. We met like we did the morning before and he explained to me that we had a very short day today and that there was only one thing on our agenda with no further explanation. We parked in a parking lot a few blocks away and I thought to myself, "Oh, great! More buildings to look at today." He told me to get out of the car and walk with him. As we walked we talked about what I saw. It felt like I was seeing things for the first time.

Then we came to a stop and that's when I noticed we were now standing in front of Chanel... I paused for just a moment to stare at the soft pink skirt suit in the front window. I looked at Albert when he opened the door and said, "After you Miss." He told me that, today we mark this off the list of how I would impact the world. Then he laughed a little. He told me a story of his mother at the track with his father and that there was always one suit she liked to wear to the races when their horses were racing. He explained to me that every woman needs one suit that made them feel powerful and today it was my turn. After buying the suit and shoes from the window I remember the feelings... unstoppable! I still remember thinking, WORLD WATCH OUT; I'M COMING...

Albert explained that we had a very important meeting the next day and that I would need to wear my new suite. Then he thanked me for a great day and that was the end of day two.

Day three; was just like any other day. We started at the White Spot restaurant where he explained to me that we were meeting with CBRE that morning. That he did business only with the President and that today he was buying a new building. I was so excited to be part of that and wow, I would get to watch him in action. I thought, "I'm going to learn so much" and I was so proud that I had bought a new notebook to match my suit. I felt ready for this experience and that I looked amazing in my new suit, I thought I was ready… but I was NOT ready for what came next.

Albert and I were guided into a large boardroom by a very nice woman about ten years my senior. She commented on how nice my suit was, it was; and it was such an amazing feeling. We were seated at the boardroom table where there were about eight different buildings all laid out on the table for us to review. Then the same women came back into the boardroom with the coffee service and asked us how we would like our coffee. She handed me my coffee cup; and I realized that I was on the other side of the cup for the very first time and at twenty-one, I couldn't believe where my life was heading. I still had no idea what would come next… Jim walked into the boardroom and welcomed Albert with a big smile. Albert introduced Jim to me with a simple smile and no explanation. We proceeded to listen to all of the benefits of each building, both from a long-term hold and cash flow perspective. I remember taking so many notes. Then we got down to the last two buildings which were the two we had looked at a few days before. At this point, Albert gets out his cheque book and filled out the payee to CBRE and signed the cheque. I remember thinking "which one did he pick." Albert then stood up and thanked Jim for all of his time, and shook his hand. I think we were both a little confused at that moment. Albert looked at me, then back at Jim and says, "Lisa will take it from here!" He looked at me and said, "I look forward to hearing all about which building you have chosen tomorrow at breakfast." He left me the blank cheque and walked out of the boardroom.

At that moment my head was spinning and I thought I was going to throw up my breakfast all over that boardroom table. I looked down and took big breath, exhaled slowly and took a sip of my coffee I looked at Jim and said, "Well, let's get started!"

We proceeded to go through the last two buildings with all of the pros and cons.

Then we started to talk about the commission rate CBRE had been taking from Mr. Zion which turned out to be five percent. I explained to Jim that they had made a lot of money from Mr. Zion over the years and that the commission rate they were charging was not acceptable to me and that he needed to do better. Jim then took a few moments to explain to me that that's the way it was. I thanked him for his time and told him that, I had chosen a building but since we could not come to terms on the commission that I would in fact, not be buying a building today. I picked the cheque up off the table, grabbed my book and purse and headed to the door, with my hands shaking and my head spinning as I reached for the door. Jim stopped me and said, "Okay, we can lower the commission to three percent." I turned back to him smiled and came back to the table. That was the day I wrote my first million-dollar cheque.

The next day Albert told me that he knew I could do it. He told me that he could see in me what I was unable to see in myself just yet. I learned that day that I was much stronger than I had ever believed I could be. I also realized that I needed to trust my gut as my intuition is rarely wrong.

I learned so many lessons from this terrific human being who mentored me for six years and wanted nothing in return other than to see me succeed and share his knowledge. I am forever grateful to the universe for giving me this great gift at a time when I was so hungry for knowledge. I am also grateful for the people in my life that keep pushing me to be better, my dad who pushes me in business, my mom who is always happy to remind me I am no better than anyone else when I'm not grounded, and my friend Erin who always pushed me to get the hell out of my comfort zone. For these people and so many more, I am extremely grateful.

Life isn't always a fairy tale... all humans have stuff! It's how we choose to show up while going through the hard times and the lessons we learn while going through the rough stuff. How we choose to move forward from there, that's what matters.

By the time I was thirty, I was successful in my own right in real estate, stocks, and money exchange, all due to the lessons I had learned from Albert. With that, I had become a little self-absorbed, to say the least. If it didn't have a label I wouldn't wear it. I only hung out with people that I perceived to have money.

Wow! Who had I become? I clearly didn't know; so the universe decided to give me a good slap in the face to remind me.

I remember not being able to get out of bed one morning not because I was tired but because "I couldn't get out of bed". I needed help to get to the doctors that morning and I was immediately sent to the clinic to have an ultrasound on what was my adrenal glands... I remember thinking; what the hell was that? Turns out they produce all of your adrenalin and cortisol.

So I'm at the ultrasound and they come in to tell me, "First of all, did you know you're pregnant? Congratulations! And you have a five-centimeter mass on one of your adrenal glands. We will send all of the results to your family doctor. He is expecting you back at his office." When I arrived back at the doctor's office he was waiting for me, which I didn't really take as a good sign. He went on to tell me that they thought I might have adrenal cancer and that the cancer clinic at KGH had already been called and they were expecting me in about an hour.... I had two thoughts at that time, "What the hell do you mean I'm pregnant? I'm so careful! And who the hell gets into the specialist in an hour?!"

I then have the second ultrasound of the day and YEP it's confirmed. I'm pregnant and yep, there is a mass of 5cm attached to the adrenal gland. It seemed to be the right shape to be cancer but because they had never had a case at the new cancer clinic in Kelowna they were going to reach out to the doctors in Vancouver for an opinion. They said that I should take the next few days to talk to my family about what was happening.

What was I going to say to my family?... maybe, kind of, they think it's possible it's cancer? So instead, I opted to tell my family that I was expecting because at that moment I thought *that* was the big, scary news.

A few days later I met my first oncologist, Dr. Onkiko, who was an exchange doctor from Japan. He had agreed to come to Kelowna and do some testing and if it tested positive he would move to Kelowna and take my case for a year and teach other doctors about a course of action and the treatments we would do. Over the next week, I got to be a human pin cushion. There was blood work daily and three more ultrasounds. At the end of that week, Dr. Onkiko and I met over coffee and he explained to me that I would have a week to decide how I was going to proceed. He told me that he would want to end my pregnancy, cut open my back and if necessary, take out my bottom rib and TRY to remove the mass in its entirety.

BUT here were the risks;

1. The surgery is long with a long recovery time and with my heart condition it would be very hard on me.

2. Once oxygen hits cancer it tends to spread if there's any left behind. Due to the fact that the adrenal gland sits near the kidneys and liver it would most likely spread there first.

3. We would be required to do chemotherapy after. Again, this could cause me to be very sick and it comes with many side effects that I needed to be aware of.

4. The odds were not in my favour. There was, at that time about twelve reported cases a year in Canada and the odds were 1 in 25 that I would make it through. I don't know what the stats are now but at that time I remember thinking, "This SUCKS!"

The last thing he said to me was, "I highly recommend that you make custody arrangements for your boys and get everything in order."

I spent the next few weeks wondering why this was happening to me? Why now? I was on top of my game. You know all of those thoughts that something is happening TO you, I played victim really well at that time. When the doctor came back I was in the darkest time in my life. But then I just got mad! I was really pissed off and I used that anger to fuel my strength over the next year.

We discussed what was the worst outcome if I didn't have the surgery. What would happen to my child if I could hang on could he survive? If I could hang on long enough to get him here safely would he be born with cancer too or could there be something wrong with him? Up to what point, could I wait until both of our lives would be in jeopardy? What point would I have to pull the ripcord? Did I have to decide today?

I had also told him that when I was in Japan years earlier I had come to learn about meditation and that their culture tried many other things first. He explained that that was not what western medicine would recommend. I told him that wasn't good enough for me and that maybe HE needed to decide how we were going to work together moving forward and that maybe HE needed a week to think about it. I remember he laughed just a little and he said, "Okay, but you're going to have to agree to do everything to the letter."

I don't really remember the things that happened next but I do remember thinking that I was going to be the one that makes it out the other side as I had things to do, like see my boys graduate and get married. This child that I was carrying was here for a reason and I would anything to protect him.

We had to make a trip to Vancouver to find a purple door in a back alley in China town in Vancouver to pick up what would be my daily routine over the next eight to ten months. It worked out to be about a hundred pills a day that I would wash down with some blended oil that tasted like dirt.

Medically, I refused to have the surgery but I did have to go about every week to have blood work done and an ultra sound weekly. We had agreed that if the mass grew to 8 cm I would have no choice but to have the surgery and proceed with the outlined medical procedures. I was losing weight like crazy, I felt like people thought I was starving to death. Being about ninety pounds on my

5'9" frame didn't help my self-image at that time. I would make jokes that I was a real-life bauble head.

It was at that point that they started to get worried, we watched cancer grow 5.3 cm, 6.1 cm, 7.4 cm and that was the last reading. I was just over six and a half months along and they had come back to me and again recommending that I follow through with the surgery, and advising that the odds of my son surviving being born were good. I had to remind them that we agreed to 8cm and that I still had time. By this point, my organs had all shifted due to the fact that there was also a baby sharing the space. They could no longer find the adrenal glands. Let's fast forward three months when I delivered a healthy son, Noah. I was taken away to start chemo just hours after delivery.

The next day I was sent for a full-body scan, the ones with the blue dye, which just about killed me as it turns out I'm allergic to it. All I could think about was, "I did not fight this hard to go out this way." They told me that they couldn't find the mass and that it seemed to be gone... No one could figure it out but they decided that they were going to do more chemo just to be sure. I had made it this far so, *bring it on,* I remember thinking. We had come out the other side.

I would never recommend going against your doctor. Clearly, mine was substantially more educated than myself and he watched intently every change medically I had. But this worked for me. As you can imagine, there is so much more to this story but I firmly believe my body, mind, soul and an unborn child fought back, and of course, I had hundreds of pills helping me along the way. This is my miracle and I will forever be grateful to the universe giving me the opportunity to be better and to do more.

During this long journey, I have learned what is happening TO me is FOR me…. teaching me what I need to know along the way. When I don't listen, it teaches me again and always a little harder than the first time. I have learned that I need to check my Ego. I'm reminded; how amazing this life is and that it can be taken at any moment. I have learned to be grateful for every moment, wins and fails, for I learn my greatest lessons when I fail.

For me, it's about the moments! When I'm gone, my family and friends won't remember the stuff… they will remember the moments we had together.

About Lisa

President Western Canada of PMA Realty Group |Community Leader | Serial Entrepreneur | Multi-Award Winning Sales Professional |Mother of six & Grandmother | Two-Time Cancer Survivor | Boss Chicks Authentic Mentor | Advisor| Professional Speaker

Lisa is a modern-day "wonder-woman"- a woman true to her word and who believes everything is possible with focus, passion and hard work. Lisa is a respected businesswoman and role model to both men and women with her exemplary work ethic, genuine desire to give back to help others achieve success and love for her family. When Lisa believes in your vision, she is the person that will help and support you at all levels expecting nothing in return. Lisa is a passionate woman who loves business, seeing challenges as gifts, and a woman who always makes time help mentor and support other women to succeed.

With over two decades of hands-on experience in both sales and management, Lisa's product knowledge expanses the globe, from projects in Panama City, Mexico and the Dominican Republic to over 5900+ condominium and new home sales in Alberta. Lisa is currently President of Western Canada for PMA Brethour Group with over 1000 new condominium and homes coming online in 2019.

Leading a successful career in the construction industry and breaking barriers in the cigar industry, successfully launching multi-franchises. Lisa started Cheap Smokes & Cigars in 2009. Now with 19 built stores in Alberta and the expansion into both British Columbia and Saskatchewan this year, Lisa is disrupting barriers and leading by example as a woman in business.

I AM a brilliant woman because I rise with more power and grace in the face of adversity.

– Lisa Mundell

I AM a Brilliant Woman

Passion is Not the Key to Success

By Deborah Janz

My toes were freezing. It was raining outside and the tent trailer that was now my home had a tear in it at the foot of the bed. I grumbled to myself that I had to move the storage bins off the other bed and into the rain so my boys, then 4 and 6, could stay with me that night. Oddly enough, I wasn't discouraged by the state of my existence. Barely 27 years old, this felt like an adventure and I was quite proud of myself for taking care of my own needs and saving money while I figured out how to get back on my feet after leaving my husband.

I had chosen the travel industry for my career path when I graduated from high school, a decision birthed from a deeply rooted desire to experience the world. When my husband and I parted ways, I had no concept of child support and was determined to take care of myself and my boys without financial assistance. Being a travel agent had served me well as a second income, but now that I was separated and struggling to afford some custody of my kids, the minimum wages from the small local travel agency that employed me were insufficient for survival.

Life got easier when I landed an account executive position with a national corporation. With a salary above the poverty line, medical benefits, car allowance, a company cell phone, and laptop, my needs were covered and the job also afforded me the time and money to attend college part-time. After two years of separation, I was finally able to house and feed my boys under my own roof, but I wasn't content.

Job security wasn't enough to feed my desire to create, to strategize and implement my ideas, to see how I could grow a business on my own and I continually juggled side projects. Among other ventures, I ran a small local wine tour company on my days off. I co-invested in a concession stand, The Sugar Shack, thinking that would be an awesome way to do something fun with my boys. (It wasn't, but that's another story.) I dabbled in network marketing, commission sales, even cash pyramid schemes. I got a rush out of working with others, inspiring and being inspired by the possibility of wealth and the lifestyle it represented.

Eventually, all my distractions cost me my job and I was forced to make a pivotal decision. Would I find another job, a more daunting proposition now that I had "fired" on my resume, or would I venture out on my own?

Opting for the flexibility of commission-only door-to-door sales jobs and working for myself seemed like a logical career focus so I could simultaneously be available for my boys. I wanted the best of both worlds: of motherhood and as a businesswoman.

The beginning of a new career

Always the techie and loving the shiny new social platform, Facebook, I leveraged my innate expertise and ventured out to offer oh-so-valuable (or so I thought) advice to small business clients. The lessons came hard and fast and ultimately, I ended up shifting from consulting, which I could not seem to get paid for, to doing the social media work for small business clients. As a pioneer in the industry, there were no models on how to do this work and I had underestimated the time requirement. Raising a couple of hungry, growing and active boys was not going to happen on the nominal income I was producing and I was working far too hard for too little.

In the meantime, my brother, Rod, and my dad had started a venture, created to offer a safe haven for children on the big scary world wide web. At that point in time, the public was beginning to see the educational value available through the internet but feared it was still primarily a pornography engine. There were few solutions for parents and "KidZap" filled that need. My dad and brother needed some help with the sales and marketing model for the subscription tool they had created, and I joined forces with them. I was back in the land of stability yet retained a certain amount of autonomy within our three-person team.

Rod and I spent long hours learning about "digital marketing", a term not yet invented to describe anything, let alone a profession. We were successful in achieving over one million views per month to our little website before Google was a thing! We worked tirelessly to educate ourselves on all there was to know about attracting clients and making money online. We thrived on the former but sucked at the latter and eventually, my dad was forced to shut down this "hobby" he was footing the bill for in order to stop his own financial bleeding.

Not learning from my dad's experience, I continued the pattern of investing in educating myself, leaping from one strategy to another, and buying subscriptions to every tool and webinar that claimed it would provide the secret potion to make money online. It's not that I believed all the claims made or even that I wanted to be a millionaire. I figured I could learn enough to provide a stable life for my kids and to fulfill my dream to travel all over the world.

The cost of not launching

I was learning a lot but never felt like I knew enough and always felt I had to work harder to satisfy the few clients I had. The tension was high as the pressure to make a liveable income forced me to work longer and harder while desperately trying to be a good mother. The fantasy of being a stay at home mom and running a business was dashed. Working from home didn't translate to baking cookies, helping with homework, and playing with Legos on the floor. My children saw me every day, but they were looking at my back as I stared at a computer, not into their beautiful eyes. It meant I was staring at bills I didn't know how to pay, and my stress was spilling over in sometimes damaging ways, to the ones I loved most.

To this day, I can't explain exactly how it happened, but the debt racked up and before I knew it, I was more than $80,000 in debt between credit cards, lines of credit, and personal loans. My brother and I were co-dependent "squirrel" traffickers. In the marketing industry, there's a shiny new object dangling in front of your face at every given moment and we were feverishly chasing them, hoping for our big break. If you already struggle to focus and are tempted by opportunities, the marketing landscape is rough terrain, full of land mines.

Confidence and Commitment: The Chicken and the Egg

Some people complain they aren't given any opportunities. As an optimist, I see opportunities everywhere! The challenge is not *finding* opportunities, but discerning which ones are worthy of investment (time, energy, and money), having the discipline to *say no* to the majority of them, and fully committing to one path for enough time that it can fulfill its promise.

Riddled with debt and still seeking a solution that would help both my customers and I be successful, I came across a digital marketing reseller program leveraging overseas contractors. I was no stranger to outsourcing overseas and was all too familiar with the challenges. It was not as simple as Tim Ferriss espoused in his best-selling book and my inspirational lifestyle guide, The Four Hour Work Week (4HWW). I would pay more for the reseller solution than if I hired contractors directly, but it would remove a lot of the aggravation of sourcing dependable talent and training them to achieve results I was struggling to achieve myself. More importantly, the training and business owner support the company provided their reselling clients, people like me, was extraordinary.

And there was an investment of $1000 to get started.

Another big decision was staring me in the face. I was at the end of my financial rope and the stress load was taking a toll on my family and my health. If this investment didn't turn things around, I would be bankrupt soon. In addition to being thoroughly embarrassed, I would be forced to get a dreaded J-O-B. I was sure I couldn't qualify for more than a minimum wage position, so it felt like a lose-lose proposition.

I bit the bullet and made a commitment to myself to be successful. This was it. I would learn from the professionals and follow their advice explicitly. My resolve was confirmed when my brother presented another enticing opportunity and I turned him down. "I know I may lose more money before I make any, but I am staying on this path now until it works," I told him. And I did.

Passion isn't enough.

You may have heard people say, "I love what I do so much that it doesn't feel like work." What an enviable position to be in! This is a worthy and achievable goal if you are a solopreneur or independent professional not interested in growing a business asset.

But passion will only take you so far if you want to grow a business that is bigger than yourself, that can run without you, that can be sold someday, and/or that requires a team in order to thrive.

Passion is not the key to entrepreneurial success. Passion leads a person to do something: bake pies, sell houses, feed the poor, decorate homes, travel the world, tutor students, crunch numbers, or whatever it is. But there are so many things you must do as an entrepreneur that will not align with your passions! Your passion may not be bookkeeping, marketing, managing people, organization of paperwork, writing contracts, etc. and yet most, if not all, of these things are required when you're an entrepreneur.

Growing a business is hard! It requires commitment, consistency, and discipline, while passion ebbs and flows. And while your passion may be strong enough at times to push you through doing those dreaded tasks, it gets challenging to sense your passion when your job shifts from doing the thing (baking pies, etc.) to being a full-time business owner. *Your commitment to the work of growing a business and resolve to stay on course must ultimately be stronger than your passion.*

My passion was and still is, making connections. I like connecting with other cultures to deeply understand our commonalities and differences. I love connecting people with resources to make their lives simpler. I love connecting people with each other. I especially love connecting a client problem with a streamlined and easily understandable strategy and execution plan. I only recently started defining my passion or my "why" in this way though.

My entrepreneurial fire was stoked early on by Tim Ferriss's vision in the 4HWW. I imagined sitting at a beachside café in Thailand with my laptop, money rolling in behind the scenes to fuel my life and dreams. I now enjoy a version of that vision, but passion alone would not have given me the persistence to get through the pains of growing a business.

Business growth and personal growth are inextricably bound.

My business was on a steady growth trajectory. Networking was a key contributor to attracting new clients and I loved the opportunity networking provided to share what I was learning along the way. Speaking to small groups not only fed the needs of attendees, but it also helped me understand the value of my expertise and all that I had learned on the bumpy road leading to each stage of growth. I was making ends meet, but I was tired of the constant hustle to land the next client. It was like applying for a job over and over and over again! However, I was honing my services and my pitch and, as my confidence increased, so did my fees. This was all good and it was simply time to level up!

A gift arrived in the form of an invitation to respond to a request for proposal from an international organization. I had no business responding to this proposal among the larger, fully staffed agencies bidding against me. I knew I would be pushing the limits of my experience and was leaping into work that was certainly over my head. I pitched "our" services and won the bid, quickly realizing that the overseas team was not going to meet the standards of this client. In a bit of a panic, I scrambled to assemble a team and services to match what I had promised and to fulfill atmospherically higher quality standards for this client.

I learned more in the following two years than I learned from a lifetime of college courses, webinars, seminars, eBooks, blogs, and podcasts combined. The contract was paying my salary and for a part-time assistant – this ONE contract, my life, so to speak, depended on it. I had to figure out how to meet the demands of this lucrative client while maintaining dozens of small clients or I had to find another way to create stability and growth. If anything went wrong with this account, I would be back to square one. The pressure was on.

Out of the comfort zone

My vision of sitting on a beach with a laptop did *not* include managing human beings. I like technology. You can boss it around and it will, for the most part, do what it is told. When your resources are limited to yourself and technology, it is clear who to blame when things go wrong. You work when it's convenient for you. In my mind, dealing with humans meant more overhead, less flexibility with time, and being responsible for someone else's livelihood when I had struggled so much to get to this place where I could pay my own bills! Furthermore, what if employees wanted to work from an OFFICE?!?!? Yuck.

So many times, I have had to leap into my discomfort to make things work. So many times, I've wanted to run away to an island and hide from the world. So many times, I have feared being exposed as an imposter in the business world. So many times, I have had to lean on discipline rather than passion to move ahead. And, it ends up, nothing prepared me for the challenge and reward of building and working with a team.

Today, I am free of all and any business and personal debt. I employ a small team of tenacious, fulltime, work-from-home employees and around a dozen North American contractors, serving service organizations across Asia, Africa, and North America. I have the freedom to travel, consult for heads of organizations around the world, speak on international stages, coach and provide masterminds for small business owners, while managing operations and I have even made room in my life for the most supportive, dream inspiring partner I could ever hope for.

The internal work of entrepreneurship largely has to do with courage, in my opinion; courage to stick with it when everyone is questioning you, the courage to make decisions without over-analyzing, the courage to commit to a plan, the courage to charge what you're worth, and the courage to take financial risks. The journey to grow a business and a lifestyle is unique for each woman brave enough to pass the starting line. How quickly each of us rises and how many twists and turns each experience depends on our ability to tackle our fears and take the next leap.

About Deborah

Deborah is a leading international branding and marketing strategist and speaker. She is recognized for delivering results-producing strategies for her clients, and utilizing an intelligent blend of creative, engaging and disruptive solutions. As a speaker, Deborah has inspired, entertained and empowered audiences with her unique ability to demystify the power of branding by integrating storytelling with the latest and most relevant technology tools.

One of her agency's unique offerings is helping organizations, with an international target audience, engage a global, highly mobile and digitized customer profile.

Deborah hails from Vancouver, BC, Canada where she enjoys spending time in the outdoors with her growing family. When not in front of business associates and clients, you will find her on a mountain trail or far below sea level, communing with sharks or turtles in a far off land.

Deborah can be reached at https://im.international

I AM a brilliant woman I can envision and activate the steps to move from struggle to success.

– Deborah Janz

I AM a Brilliant Woman

A Resilient Backbone

By Sloane Hunter

The "resilient backbone" - a metaphor for life. It means to have the strength and stability in life, like a strong spine, to weather the short-falls, despite failures, while still moving forward. It is being able to hold the long-term vision and perspective in life that holds you together during disappointment or tragedy, so as to not crumble at the drop of circumstances. But at the same time, like a healthy spine, one needs the flexibility to bend or adapt as needed to adjust or shift ones' perspectives and expectations in order to remain resilient to the things in life that are out of our control.

In this chapter, I hope to share three influential times in my life that have all shaped the kind of person I am today and how they have made me the kind of chiropractor I never knew I could be.

I was walking down the wobbly and bumpy sidewalks of Venice with my girlfriends on a post-graduation backpacking trip in 1999. My parents had just informed me by phone that I got accepted into THE coveted Canadian chiropractic school, after having jumped through all kinds of hoops in the application process. To my surprise, rather than feeling elation with the words of acceptance, I felt stress, anxiety, and concern! Wasn't this what I WANTED? Little did I know that in the few months prior, the choices I made then would shape the trajectory of my entire career. You see, not only did I visit the school in Toronto in the fall prior, but I was also fortunate to connect to the son of an acquaintance who was studying chiropractic down in Iowa. On a whim, I decided to expand my cross-country College tour, and in the process of opening myself up to opportunities that were not on my initial radar, the journey shaped my choices.

I've anguished over doing what I wanted or *should* do and what I grew to feel I wanted in my heart more. The struggle in life is often not allowing oneself to adapt and follow these feelings ENOUGH to take the leap and let go of the "idea" of the right journey and allowing oneself to define the journey as they go. I certainly didn't have my life planned out from an early age, and when you're a people pleaser, the desire to not let others down can be a strong influence. For me, this choice in schools felt epic at my young age, as the logical and obvious choice was to stay in Canada, rather than choose to move to an American College situated on the Mississippi River in Iowa. I literally had to look up Iowa on a map to find out where it was! But looking back at my journey, I can see how every opportunity, every step, every difficulty was essential in my growth.

At the University of Alberta, I studied the physiology of exercise and physical movement (Kinesiology). I started to solidify my understanding of health and that the body *adapts* to the demands placed on it. The S.A.I.D. principal means *"Specific Adaptation to Imposed Demand",* which essentially means that your health is largely in your control, by your choices. Genetics is really only a small piece of our health expression and it is the lifestyle (or demands or lack thereof) that we place on the body that affects how we function, age and evolve. So, rather than waiting for sickness to set it, I was inspired at the idea of teaching others what they CAN do to regain and/or preserve their health. The exercise phrase "use it or lose it" is widely used, but it is essentially the essence of health preservation for long-term function. I also grew to realize that health was defined not by how you FEEL but by what you can DO (as in functional capacity). Medication can cover an ache or pain and bring relief but am I really expressing true health if I am dependent on covering up this body signal? What if I feel good but actually have undiagnosed hypertension or heart disease? Symptoms do not represent a good picture of healthiness, and the goal of "health" care should not be to just eliminate these symptoms. These simple questions had me searching for a profession that focuses more on function restoration as a solution to failing health.

I found the choice to be a chiropractor quite easy as I was nearing my undergrad degree, I just had no idea how diverse and broad this profession could be. As a whole, it is a profession that seeks to educate the public to look within themselves for health answers. It helps people feel better by getting them to function better, which is beyond just the removal of symptoms. I wanted control in my schedule and to be my own boss. I wanted to feel like I was inspiring people to live their best life (thank you, Oprah, for that phrase!). I knew that *form* and *function* of the body work hand in hand, so in simple terms, if you exercise a crooked spine, you only strengthen a crooked spine. And the better the form, the more stable, flexible and comfortable it can innately become.

Choosing my school, however, was not so easy. Each school offered different techniques and different philosophies of practice. Iowa was definitely not on my radar and living in the mid-west was not my idea of a good time. However, when I made my visit to see each campus, I felt a buzz at Palmer College of Chiropractic (they call it "Spizz") that I'd never felt anywhere else. I soon found out that it was the fountainhead of the profession and being there had me feeling like I was part of something important and historical. It was the source of the dread that I felt in Europe... because my mind felt I SHOULD stay in Canada, but my heart was at Palmer. I had to follow my heart, and once I did, I never looked back.

I learned to feel my inner guidance and pay attention to opportunities that would come up when I would set an intention. I firmly believe that people, events and alternate opportunities present themselves at the perfect time when you set an intention. But it's not only paying attention that matters but it's also being willing to take action. You need to be willing to follow a feeling, to trust that the solution will become clear and the feelings will confirm it.

Here I was at twenty-two years old and on an absolute high from the 3-month journey across Europe while gaining clarity on my career path. Then my whole world crashed down the day after I returned. The police came to my family's house and I remember the wailing of my mother as I passed the family room window. I realized something really bad had happened. As I entered the house, another officer intercepted me until I heard the truth... my older brother Chris was dead. My only sibling, my biggest fan and protector, had tragically died that morning on a lead climb up a mountain in Canmore, Alberta. The timing of my arrival home was uncanny and yet unbelievably fortunate, having just arrived home a mere twenty-four hours prior. It made the experience of hearing the news more surreal and foggier. I felt out-of-body and was literally witnessing myself go through all the initial stages of grief like an outsider. Time stood still in that house as I was in shock and disbelief, then denial and eventually sadness interchangeable with numbness... I didn't see the meaning and lesson behind this one and as the days moved on, I started to question how I was going to pick up and move on? Though I was essentially an adult, the thought of living the rest of my life "alone" without my brother, making me now an "only child" in an instant was unbelievably painful. The funeral was that week and to top it off, I was asked to compose and present his eulogy. I don't remember what I said or how I created it but it felt as though I was held up by something bigger than myself and I allowed it to guide me. At the funeral, all I know was that everyone applauded me for a tremendous and emotional sharing to honour my brother's life. All through my grieving, I instinctually allowed the emotions of feeling lost and broken but it was amplified by also having to witness the horror of seeing my parents' grief as they processed the loss of their first-born child.

This life-changing experience forced me to keep the big picture of life in mind. With time, I realized that this tragedy provided many gifts and it is with this mindset and wisdom, that I regularly teach the patients I see in my practice. I grew to appreciate my own resilience and survivorship in this life. I also gained a greater life perspective, which gives me the ability to release and let go of my constant need to control circumstances. I saw how time presses forward and how each day brings value to a healing journey. I learned how to hold compassion and patience for myself so as not to force or push away from the hurt in the process. It had me recognize the fragility and impermanence of life and in doing so, other life stresses can be faced without the same degree of overwhelm. When I understood how little time we have in this life, I could keep being grateful for the things going "right" in my life as opposed to dwelling on the "hard" parts. And due to the experience, I've grown to appreciate and be in awe of the spectrum and magnitude of our human emotion. When we can remember that we are all here only for a finite amount of time, the ability to face the future and say "YES" to change, becomes not only digestible but invited. Embracing an ever-changing journey, we can continue moving forward by being adaptable and resilient in life. This is really the only choice we have.

Fast forward to me in my forties. After a couple practice moves and three children later, I can attest to some other personal conflicts and realizations in the new "modern-day ideal" of striving for a woman's career success, growth, and development. The conflict began with the addition of our three boys over the course of 6 years all the while trying to sustain a thriving practice. The focus on my career was suffering as I strived to achieve a balance in family and work. I often felt shame and guilt throughout the past decade on both sides. Guilt that I didn't hold the same growth and momentum every year in practice, as compared to my "non-mom" female colleagues or male counterparts. Guilt for not being present to my children in their early years as I was often multi-tasking at home. This is a modern-day issue for many career women I know and certainly does not have an easy solution.

"We expect women to hold careers as if they don't have children and raise children as if they don't have careers".

THIS is the modern work/career struggle for women. It highlights the discrepancy between what I've given up for having family and the growth in my career that I know I could achieve. It has weighed on me over the years and the pressure to "have it all" has become more imprisoning than freeing. I chose to stay home for 3.5 months after each child and returned to practice part-time. I have remained so, for the sake of this work-life balance. Some ask, "When are you going back to full-time practice"? Conversely, some speak about home school and why my kids would thrive better and stay home as long as possible as time is so short when kids are small. Many of my male colleagues have stay-at-home wives who have the primary role of caring for the home. I know my career choice has also limited the success and growth of my husband's career, as we both truly "co-parent" to make it work. Through all this confusion and mixed messages in society, I have learned to focus on what *I* define as success in this modern world.

There are many forms of how a career can take shape yet many seek high volume production, employing multiple practitioners and practice locations. Some see success as traveling to every conference and attending every speaking opportunity to share their message of a healthy lifestyle. But when I have other priorities at home, these goals and focuses become too taxing and comparing to others' life and standards is simply torture and nothing to strive for. I choose to live my own unique journey and focus on what gives me meaning each day. We all have an impact on the world around us. I choose the work/life balance that allows me to wake up in the morning and know I can make a lasting impression on the world, one person at a time, with quality, sincerity, and attention.

B.J. Palmer, the developer of chiropractic, once said: "You never know how far-reaching something you think, say or do will affect the lives of millions tomorrow". I see this as the ripple effect. The extent of influence of that one drop in the still water is unknown… the point is to be a ripple. My heart is content knowing that I can make a ripple in the water of life. I don't need to be a crashing wave to be the change but through each connection, I know I can inspire and influence other lives and still come home to be there wholly for my family. And if I can stay on this personal journey with the best of intentions, even amongst the home chaos of night-time vomits and day time battles, I have succeeded to make my life worthwhile.

I hope this chapter will leave you with the realization that life isn't easy, but it is worth every challenge and experience. Remain open to the guidance in life, which can lead you to better opportunities, and marvel at the spectrum of human emotion from the deepest sorrow to extreme elation. Figure out what serves you in happiness, not what others define for you. Allow every experience to help you to grow perspective on what's really important and still dive in. That is LIVING and SUCCESS!

About Sloane

Dr. Sloane Hunter has been offering NUCCA spinal care to the city of Calgary since 2003 after graduating from Palmer College of Chiropractic in Davenport, Iowa. She became fully trained in the NUCCA spinal evaluation and corrective procedures before graduating Magna Cum Laude. Dr. Hunter also earned a Bachelors of Physical Education & Recreation (Kinesiology) at the University of Alberta in 1998 where her studies centered on Active Living for the older adult.

She maintains membership with the National Upper Cervical Chiropractic Association (NUCCA) and serves as a board member on the Ralph R Gregory Memorial Foundation (Canada), which supports the Research, Education, Endowment and Public Awareness of the NUCCA procedure in Canada. She has broadened her scope of practice with the International Chiropractic Pediatric Association (ICPA), which specifically trains practitioners to address the specific structural issues for women in pregnancy, both pre and postnatal, and in the pediatric population. She currently holds certification with the ICPA for the Webster Technique.

Dr. Hunters' husband is a Doctor in Traditional Chinese Medicine, and together they keep a healthy balance at home or outdoors with their three sons, Leighton, Calvin & Marshall.

More information about her practice can be found at hunterspinalcare.com.

I AM a brilliant woman because I embrace the challenges, the changes, the unknown, the known, the sadness and joys of life, and with the knowledge that every facet on this journey has a meaningful purpose to a full life experience!

– Sloane Hunter

I AM a Brilliant Woman

Behind the Mask

By Janice Kendall

I am almost sixty years young. I feel like I only started enjoying being alive twelve years ago and I now know this amazing journey will continue until I leave this earth. It was a difficult and painful first forty-eight years that lead me to a new and much happier path.

In my late forties, something drastically changed for me. It sounds a bit cliché but my spirit awakened to God, higher power or whatever terminology you use. I say, God.

I have so much to be grateful for. In truth, I'm now able to be grateful. I have a loving daughter, grandson, and son-in-law. My mother is eighty-nine and still healthy and enjoying her life. I have a circle of wonderful friends and a great man in my life. I also co-own a successful business. I am truly blessed.

However, looking back over my childhood, teenage years and most of my adulthood, I was living under a dark cloud. I could come out from under there for short periods of time but I could not sustain it. I always ended up back under that cloud.

I'm not sure why that was the case. My parents provided financial abundance for my two sisters and me. I know they loved me although, even in my childhood, my father and I had a very volatile relationship. But I will dive more into that later.

I remember being only six or seven years old. My bedroom faced the backyard and there was a big weeping willow tree. The birds would chirp in that tree from sunrise to sunset and I couldn't stand it. To me, it was noisy and unpleasant. I think now, how odd it is that as a child I could be annoyed by the sound of birds chirping.

I had several odd behaviours as a child. I would bite my knuckles until they bled, I would hyperventilate at bedtime worrying about being able to fall asleep and I also had a weird facial tic. Things like this continued into my teenage years and even my twenties.

As I said earlier I know now my parents did their best. However, my dad had a very difficult time dealing with my quirky personality. Even from early childhood, I think he was frustrated and disappointed with me. This resulted in him seeming very angry. Sometimes he would be verbally cruel and sometimes he would strike me. Then later he would come to me and try to be gentle and talk and even hug me. As I look back now, it really confused me. It was a love/hate relationship. But as a child I did not understand that my dad was battling his own demons.

I realize many children had far worse experiences in their childhood with their parents than this. The reason I'm sharing this information is that because of this roller coaster ride of emotions with my father, my personality was shaped in many ways that didn't serve me well as an adult,

Several behaviours surfaced in my twenties and even flowed over into my thirties; heavy drinking, promiscuity, self-sabotage and a lot of anger resulting from not liking or loving myself. However, the biggest result of my difficult relationship with my dad was that I really did not like or trust men. Male energy repulsed me for many years,

I had two short marriages by the time I was thirty-one. I also had a beautiful baby girl with my second husband. My first marriage lasted eighteen months and my second only lasted three years. Both of these men were good men. They both were kind and generous. My daughter's father continues to be a good and loving father through to this day.

I think I was afraid to be really seen. I thought "who could love me? So I would leave before they would see the real me. I was very attractive and seemed very confident but that confidence was an act in those days. So attracting men was easy but staying in a relationship was very difficult.

Finally, at about age forty-two, I just gave up. I decided a loving relationship just wasn't for me. Around that time my daughter came to live with me full time and I just isolated myself and tried my best to be a mom. I wasn't always so great at it. I had a lot of anger and was still drinking a lot. Unfortunately, my daughter had to live through that with me. She is 28 now and we have talked about all of this. She loves me and forgives me and we have a great relationship now.

So let us skip ahead to 2007. Things are about to change. This is the year I woke up and slowly started on a new and different path.

I had been invited to attend an Executive Women's International event. The speaker was Elisabeth Fayt. As she spoke something inside, my intuition, said, "You need to learn more from this woman". She mentioned, during her talk, that she ran workshops and I just knew I had to attend one. The next day I contacted Elisabeth and she had one opening left in her workshop that was starting the following week. I took that spot and it was the beginning of my new journey.

Elisabeth had written a book called "Paving It Forward". It was all about the Law of Attraction. What we think about and how we speak it is what we attract into our lives. Well for many people this was an old concept. For me, this was brand new and I needed to learn all I could.

So she gently took me through a process over the next several weeks towards some self-awareness. I truly believed my unhappiness and anger was caused by unpleasant circumstances and by other people's behavior towards me. I was a "blamer". Her soft nature eventually guided me to a place of taking responsibility for my own happiness. She said, "happiness is a choice". At first, this made me angry. This meant I had to change the way I looked at things. Instead of changing the people and circumstances, I had to look inside and change me. Change how I perceived things. I had to choose whether I wanted to be happy or unhappy. What a concept! It took me 6 months to understand and believe this. But as I learned more and took slow steps to change my thinking I got happier. It actually worked.

During the workshop, someone had ordered a book from Elisabeth but had decided not to purchase it. She asked if anyone would like to buy it and without hesitation, I said that I'd take it. It was called "Where There Is Light" by Paramahansa Yogananda. This book resonated with me like nothing else ever had. I spent the next year reading many of Yogananda's books and ordered his weekly lessons. I learned how to meditate, how to love and appreciate myself and how to shift my thinking from the negative to more positive. I found moments of true peace for the first time in my life.

About a year after taking the workshop I met Karen Klassen. I was going through a difficult time with some of the dynamics at our company. At that time, my father was an investor and shareholder so I was interacting with him much more then I had in the past twenty years. I was really struggling, so I hired Karen and took her coaching program. However, instead of seeing her once a week we did the speedy version and I was seeing her three times a week.

I still had a lot of anger towards my dad. I had worked hard on forgiveness and loving him through meditation and prayer but the real turning point was in a regression session with Karen. I found myself in a cave with my father, he was a little boy around five or six years old.

My father's childhood story is heart-breaking one. He was born and lived in a small town in Denmark. He never knew his biological father. He lived with his mother and his half-sister that was nine years older than him. When he was five his mother met a man and he said he would marry her but she had to get rid of her son. So she ran an advertisement in the local paper, putting my dad up for adoption. A family came and met him and one day they just took him away to live with them. There was no explanation given to him. He was just given away and started a new, different life in a neighbouring town.

So here I am, in that cave watching this play out and all I could think about was, what if that was my daughter Devon; how would I feel. I began to weep. I fell in love with this sweet little boy, this wounded little child – my dad. This was a pivotal moment in my life. All my anger and resentment towards my dad left me. I felt love, forgiveness and deep compassion for him.

When this happened my father was seventy-eight years old. Now when I spent time with him I was kinder and more loving. I was much happier than at any time in my life and my dad saw the change. One day I was sitting in the car with him outside my business and he looked at me with tears in his eyes said, "You've changed. What have you done? I want what you have." We cried together and I realized just how deeply I loved him.

I explained to him that I had started on a new path in life. I gave him books to read and recommended he take a coaching program with Karen Klassen, which he did and really enjoyed. He would leave his sessions whistling. Unfortunately, his dementia began to worsen quite quickly so he only had a short time of trying to change before his focus and memory would not allow him to go any further with it.

From that time on he and I became very close. My dad's health failed over the next several years and he ended up in a care facility for the last six months of his life. I visited him almost every day. One day, while watching golf together in his room, he took my hand, looked into my eyes and told me how much he loved me and how proud he was of me. My father had never said anything like this to me, ever in my life.

I was with him when he passed. I was holding his feet in my hands and looking directly into his eyes when he took his last breath. It was such a privilege to be with him at that moment. I sobbed and sobbed. It was bittersweet because I knew he wanted to die as he was in a lot of pain but I knew I would miss him.

This experience with my dad created a shift in how I wanted to feel about men. I had a grandson. A sweet little baby boy and I wanted to love him completely, including his male energy.

I started to slowly shift my misguided feelings towards men. I realized by never being in a truly loving relationship with a man, I was missing out on growing as a woman and as a human being. This shift did not happen overnight; it actually took about three years. I eventually worked with Christine Hart, a love coach. I had heard her speak at Karen's retreat and once again something in her talk resonated with me. We worked together for several months. She helped me to understand men better and to be more open to their energy. Instead of being repelled my male energy as I had done for years, I began to embrace it.

As I learned to embrace male energy, I realized I was uncomfortable with my femininity and that I had been for years. I saw being feminine as being weak. When I would observe women changing their demeanor when a man entered the conversation – it really bothered me. I couldn't understand why they would do this. On this journey to find a loving partner I softened and allowed myself to start being feminine. To try it out. Now, I really enjoy it. It is apparent to me in how I dress, walk and especially how I interact with men now. I am proud to be a feminine woman.

I had tried online dating on and off for about five years. Literally, only five dates in five years. None of them went past three or four dates. I was making progress, but very slowly. I remember saying to Christine in one of our sessions that I want to meet a man the old fashion way. Face to face. I asked God for this and about 8 months later I did meet a man. In person, face to face. He is kind and loving. I still fall back into old patterns of thought sometimes, but now I have the self-awareness and tools to get back on track again.

I want to be very honest and say I still struggle with anger. In writing my story I realized that I had let my discipline in this area slip a bit in the last few years. I want to be authentic, so this really made me take a closer look at myself. I'm choosing to be calm, peaceful and happy. So yes, I have the awareness and the tools; but it means nothing without practice. I have recommitted to practice daily and to making it more key in my life. Knowing things and practicing them is not the same. When Karen asked if I would write my story for this book, I really struggled with saying yes. I guess I knew I had to realign parts of my life and make some shifts; so these words would ring true – true to me.

Karen has been a gift to me. She started as my coach and through the years we have become friends. She still teaches me. Just spending time with Karen is an opportunity to learn. She shares her wisdom with an open and loving heart. She has helped so many people move from suffering and pain to living a happy and fulfilling life.

I remember years ago at that workshop with Elisabeth; she asked me to make a list of ten strengths or things I liked about myself. I could not list one that I genuinely believed. Twelve years later I most definitely can.

I am generous

I am loyal

I am smart

I am funny

I am a good mother

I am caring

I am feminine

I am compassionate

I am a good friend

I am kind

The journey of learning and trying to be my best will continue until I die. God has surrounded me with wise friends and teachers. I can say with honesty that I am grateful for this wonderful life.

One: Inclusion of others can make such a difference in someone's day or even life. We have all been at a cocktail party where people form a circle in conversation. Inclusion is as simple as opening up that circle to a person standing alone. We all want to feel connected and worthwhile. In social situations just be aware of the people around you. Let everyone feel they are special and included. Even if it's just for a short moment of time, be present and aware with others. This small act could help someone to feel great.

Two: Forgive yourself when you slide back or make a mistake. When you become aware of the error; start at that moment to face it, feel it and then change. Don't beat yourself up about it; be kind and loving to yourself as you would be to a friend. Life is about growing and changing. Negative emotions are a gift from God to steer us in the right direction. If we feel a negative emotion don't dwell on it, just deal with it. Emotions exist to let us know where we are. If it feels bad, we need to change something. If it feels good, we are going the right way.

Three: Connecting with God is my key to all happiness. Meditation is the most powerful tool I have to changing and growing. Talking to God throughout the day in casual conversations also makes me feel more connected to myself. I read uplifting books and surround myself with positive friends. As I started on a spiritual path a lot of my old friends naturally dropped away and new friends with similar ideals and desires appeared. I am very thankful for my girlfriends.

PS. I now love the sound of birds chirping.

About Janice

I consider myself a Calgarian. I have lived here since I was five years old.

I am Co-owner of Jerome's Appliance Gallery with Jerome Curran. We sell high-end residential appliances and have been in business for thirteen years. We pride ourselves on offering exceptional customer service. We have a beautiful showroom in Fisher Park and feature a live Bistro where a chef cooks lunch for our staff and clients every day. We have weathered two recessions and are still here and thriving.

I am a mother, grandmother, daughter, and sister. I love my family very much. My girlfriends are a big part of my life. Through them, I find love, wisdom, and fun. They are very important to me.

Karen Klassen has been key in helping me change my life. I'm so thankful she is my coach and my friend.

I AM a brilliant woman because I know how to bring the right people together to accomplish great things.

– Janice Kendall

I AM a Brilliant Woman

On The Day I Was Born

By Nirmala Naidoo

On the day I was born, I was born with fewer rights than millions of other human beings on the planet. Because of skin colour, my family and families like mine were seen as racially inferior.

My story began in South Africa, under the oppressive, institutionalized racial segregation system of Apartheid. Families like mine, people who had done nothing other than being born with skin that could withstand the sun in the places where they evolved, were punished for skin colour. We could not eat in certain restaurants, swim at certain beaches, or vote.

My family left South Africa because my parents didn't want to raise their children in a place where we weren't considered equal. We moved here to Canada when I was just two-years-old. But I vowed at a young age never to take human rights for granted: because unlike many, I know first-hand what it's like NOT to have them. Human rights are the first rights we need to live, learn, earn a living and to thrive happily and with dignity. Without them - we have nothing.

I am a veteran journalist, a public figure, a politician, a mother, and a wife. But I also have a unique perspective on life because I'm a minority on two fronts: I'm a woman... AND I'm a visible minority.

When talking about human rights, women's rights are sometimes seen as separate. But they are not. As Hilary Clinton has said, "Women's rights are human rights and human rights are women's rights."

One thing that's becoming clear in this day and age, is that the clock can be turned back on many things we thought were safe. Human rights and women's rights cannot be taken for granted. Complacency is our enemy.

I entered the field of journalism because of my passion for human rights. I wanted to be the voice for those who didn't have one and for those who didn't know they had one. I wanted to be a catalyst for change by telling their stories. And I witnessed powerful stories that reaffirmed my commitment to make lives better.

When I worked as a journalist in London, England – during and after the first Gulf War... I recall doing a story on homelessness. I had arranged to spend the day with two homeless men I had met the day before. When I arrived, I entered a dark tunnel under a train bridge and was greeted by the two men who then proceeded to introduce me to their parents, their siblings, children, and friends – all of whom came crawling out of these dark, spaces overhead. I was shocked. These weren't just homeless people – these were homeless families - it was a homeless community. But even more shocking – was the fact that the dark tunnel was illuminated by an open fire with a huge, bubbling pot hanging over it. IN that pot – was a chicken curry they had made for me – pulled together by foraging for scraps of food. I remember thinking – if people with so little can be so willing to give so much, how can we not do the same? It became a mantra for my life.

Also in London, I recall doing a British election story for Christian Science Monitor about a radical fringe party called the British National Party.

I reached out to the party to ask if I could interview the leader for a story that would air in the United States on our network. After thinking about it for three days, they said: "Yes, we'll do it because we want to tell Americans what we're about". But they also said "You need to understand two things before we do the interview: First – we are racist in the fullest sense of the word. And secondly, we will not be interviewed by anyone who is not white." The sting of those words was sharp. Not only was it an affront to me as a journalist, but it was also a disheartening reminder that blatant racism and discrimination was alive and well out in the open, devoid of any shroud of shame. I'm happy to say that my network chose not to do the interview, stating, "no one will tell us which of our journalists will or will not interview them and we will not give a platform to hatred."

I remember doing a story on Global Television years ago. I got a call from a distraught father whose teenager had run away from home and eventually called him to say goodbye because she'd just learned she had AIDS and was dying on the streets of Vancouver. I hopped on a plane with a photographer, pounded the pavement for three days — and saw things no human being should ever see. Brothels, drug houses, despair, addiction, blood. Eventually, we found the teen in a crack house. She came out of the house, saw me and turned to runaway — wary that we might be police officers. And this is where being a woman kicked in for me — as a woman myself, I had the forethought to consider what would appeal to a young, troubled woman like Amy — as a woman myself. I had taken with me photographs of the children she'd had as a younger teen who were given up for adoption. And I said, "Amy, I have photos of your children". She stopped, turned around and walked over to me, and crumpled into a ball at my feet sobbing. We interviewed her and by the end of our time together, she was begging me to bring her home. We contacted agencies to help reunite her with her family. Years later, she was clean, sober and invited me to her wedding.

After twenty-seven years as a journalist, I realized the same stories kept coming up. The names would change, some of the details would differ — but the stories simply wouldn't go away. I reported stories not just because truth matters, but because I wanted the world to see injustices and be compelled to take action. But soon I realized it wasn't enough to tell stories and HOPE someone would do something about it — I needed to move to politics to MAKE change happen.

Running in the 2015 Federal Election was one of the best things I've ever done. The experience was invaluable. I learned so much – about myself, about people, and about politics.

The main thing that I learned, was how many people don't realize the true "power of one". They don't realize their voice, their vote, and their actions can change the world. Maybe not all at once, but in small ways that can make a huge impact.

First, I'm shocked by how many women during the election said "I don't care about politics" or I'll give this to my husband and he can decide how we'll vote. Women have only had the right to vote since the 1960s in Canada, and many are already giving that right away!

In the 2015 election, everyone was talking about the niqab issue. They were talking about whether women should be allowed to wear them in CEREMONIAL – not legal – citizenship ceremonies. The issue came to the forefront after one woman who fought for her personal right to wear one.

I was outspoken about the niqab issue, arguing that if women want to wear them, they should be allowed to make that decision themselves. And then - in one of my debates during the election – a man wearing a confederate flag on his face showed-up, saying he was there because of the pro niqab stance I was taking, and that someone was going to get hurt. The building was surrounded by police, they whisked us out of the room and the suspect was arrested.

The day after the incident, I had a conversation with Former Prime Minister, Joe Clark's wife, Maureen McTeer – who said,

"This conversation is being led mostly by men in politics. Men should NOT be telling women how to dress." She was right.

One of the biggest assaults on human rights comes from language. Words matter and truth matters. In these modern times, people all too often feel brazen enough to voice racist, misogynistic and hateful things. We are living in a fast-paced world where social media and biased sources of news can give center stage to assaults on truth and human rights by sowing the seeds of hate, fear, and division.

Increasingly, we have to be vigilant about not sliding down the slippery slope into undoing decades of human rights triumphs. Rhetoric isn't just rhetoric. The rhetoric that's divisive appeals to the worst in people, incites hate and feeds paranoia. We are seeing an erosion of the checks and balances, stigma and barriers that make hate unacceptable. And that means we are increasingly permitting it. We are witnessing xenophobia, white nationalism, and antisemitism in ways we've never seen before in our lifetime. That's not an accident. That is what happens when you remove the stigma of division and hate speech and allow hatred to grow unchecked

Who would have thought in the 21st century: after the work of Mahatma Gandhi, Martin Luther King, Malala Yousefzai, and Nelson Mandela, after freedom to marry whomever you want, after women got the vote and all the other things that make democracy great --- that we'd be witnessing a collective unease in the world today. Why? Because despite all our freedoms and successes, we are seeing a movement against immigration, brazen

Neo-Nazism, a resurgence of victim shaming, and bullying of brave women in the public eye.

Throughout history, there have been movements to correct the injustices in the world and we thought we had them beat for the most part. But in the 21st century, when we thought the world was finally a place where our children wouldn't have to fight for much more, we are seeing what some would argue is a regression.

Human rights cannot be taken for granted. Ever. From the poverty I witnessed in my career, to child prostitution, to racism, to a woman's right to wear what she wants, we need to speak out each and every time. My call to action in these modern times is to adopt a zero-tolerance for Intolerance.

We are all people of influence, especially in the era of social media. Stand up and use your voices to fight for human rights every single time. It's easy to quietly take offense to human rights abuses, but if you don't speak up, your silence is as good as agreeing with it. Nelson Mandela said it best: "Fools multiply when wise men are silent".

Our voices matter. We cannot sit on the side-lines and hope someone else steps up. We need to preserve what all those who came before us fought so hard for; freedom, acceptance, equality, civility, and compassion.

In this world of alternative truths, experimentation, fear, and division – each of US is the answer. Be informed, be brave, be loud.

About Nirmala

Nirmala Naidoo is a veteran award-winning television anchor and journalist who was declared "a person of extraordinary ability" by the United States Government. She has worked for CTV's W5, NBC London, Christian Science Monitor Television (London), Visnews London, Middle East Broadcasting (London) and was the suppertime anchor for Global Calgary and CBC Calgary. By using journalism to tell their stories, she is an outspoken advocate and keynote speaker for human rights issues, fighting for the rights of minorities, immigrants, victims of bullying, and those who are marginalized or powerless by using journalism to tell their stories. Nirmala is a former politician as the 2015 Federal Election Political Candidate for the Liberal Party of Canada for Calgary Rocky Ridge. She is also a former Keynote Speaker for Enbridge's Famous Five, made Calgary's Top 40 Under 40 list twice, is named one of the 150 Women Who Shaped Alberta, and was on the cover of TIME Magazine.

I am a brilliant woman trying to make a difference.

– Nirmala Naidoo

I AM a Brilliant Woman

A Pinch of bliss – Sprinkle and Sparkle

By Nicole Stettler

I had this misconception that the only way to connect with my audience is to touch them through hardship and pain. But this definitely is not the case. We can choose to maximize on the negatives in our lives or we can choose to feel blessed and turn all of these negatives into positives. And this is how I'm going to begin the rest of my story.

I'm actually standing here at this very moment rather speechless (in almost disbelief) realizing that, "Oh my God, it's really happening. I really made it." I have actually already written my chapter. I spent hours and minutes and days and nights thinking about what I should write and how I should write it and actually writing and sending it to the editor saying that it was complete. And then I had an "ah-ha" moment this morning. My chapter was filled with sadness and sorrow and self-pity and stories of myself climbing out of holes of darkness. Then I thought why am I am embracing all of this negativity. I believe more than anyone that life is about choices. I don't want to choose to share sad moments of my life in order to connect with someone. This should not be the way that we look at life. We don't need to come from somewhere dark in order to be someone bright. We can choose to only think of the positives, remember the negatives but they don't need to depict how life goes.

I Am Successful.

To say that out loud brings tears to my eyes. I actually have tears rolling down my cheeks at this very moment in all honesty. As many of you know running your own business and choosing this path is not the easiest choice that life has to offer. But in doing so the pride that I take when I tell someone what I do and how I got here is absolutely priceless.

Every single day is a challenge I'm not going to lie to you. Some days I wake up and think wow I have it all under control all the laundry is clean my car is washed my kids are in school my staff is working and I'm planning my trip to British Columbia next weekend. Then the next day it seems like everything is falling apart. It's a constant struggle, the roller coaster is real. That's the life of an entrepreneur who wants it all. Nothing amazing happens overnight. Making the decision to hold your own, to take the responsibility of supporting your staff and helping them have successful lives, to build your empire is something I believe only a few people are able to do. I have an endless fire within me. This is a blessing and a curse at the same time. Some days I wake up and think it's a curse and that's when the real challenge happens. These are the days I have to remind myself that I am blessed, that I am strong, that I am powerful, and that I am doing all that I am doing for my beautiful children.

Everyone has their own driving force and mine is definitely 100% the fact that I personally have the power to give my children anything they want. Perhaps this is because I never felt that I received this from my parents. Perhaps this feeling comes from elsewhere. I'd rather not elaborate on this because I want to stay positive. The whole message I want to pass on is we can make our future. We can wake up and set our intentions. We can manifest our goals and dreams. Emphasizing on the negative in the hurdles that we have overcome in our lives in my opinion only holds back the true power and strength that we have within ourselves.

I Am A Real Person.

I have gone through struggles. I am divorced and a single mother of two. I basically started my business out of my garage. I have zero post-secondary education when you refer to college and university. I have certifications on top of certifications when it comes to fitness training, nutrition, aesthetics', skin anatomy. Basically, anything that I felt passionate about I pursued. When I decided to leave my marriage I left with $1000. I walked away from our perfect home and our perfect family because I just wasn't fulfilled. I knew that I was going to be okay and that I could do anything I wanted. I knew I had the work ethic. I wasn't above any job that would cross my path or too proud to scrub toilets. I would do what I had to do to get to the goal that I had, no matter what it took. I have determination. This is a characteristic that I take great pride in because it differentiates me from others in a positive way. Being humble from the heart is a characteristic that I have also been blessed with and that has helped me on my journey.

My journey as an entrepreneur had been started very young in my life. I was raised in a family that was forced to start a home business. At eleven years old I was responsible for cleaning an entire government building after school before any outdoor play was allowed. At the time I dreaded this job my father had put in place and didn't understand why all the other kids were allowed to play. I didn't quite understand that this would one day immensely impact who I am today. I wanted my children to do the same, even though I said I would never make my children do this kind of work at such a young age. An example like this shows you that you can teach your children positive leadership skills, confidence, and strength. Again, I'm making a choice to see the good rather than the bad in that childhood situation.

Every day that I wake up I set a goal. First, I make my bed because I once heard that when you start your day doing something as simple as making your bed you have started your day on a path of success. I truly believe this statement because I leave my room and look back and admire the fact that I have earned such a simple thing as a beautiful bed in a beautiful home. I try not to take the little things for granted. My background is a Costa Rican descent and growing up my parents did a very good job of showing me my heritage and taking me overseas to really appreciate what we have here in Canada that others don't have. I think one of the most important things about becoming successful is to stay humble. Little things like flushing your toilet paper in the toilet bowl because we have a proper sewer system, the ability to have hot water every day in our showers, almost everyone having access to their own vehicle, and being able to take the time to drive my children to school; these are all things that people take for granted but really we should step back and look at these examples and appreciate that this is our life. Therefore, not only do I look back at my bedroom in the morning, I also look at my home, my car and pictures of my family on the wall and all of our memories and say thank you in my heart. I take pride in myself for being this way and I am grateful to my parents for raising me to see the difference. Then I can set my day, I can be strong and ready for all the challenges that I have chosen for myself. I can accomplish my list of daily goals. And most of all I can get closer to the life goals and career goals that I have set for myself.

Life is hard and it's tough trying to stay positive ALL of the time. There are three main points that I like to call gems that I want to share with you. These three gems are what have empowered me in becoming the strong woman that I am.

Gem #1 BELIEVE IN YOURSELF

Self-doubt hides everywhere. It hides behind every shadow and every corner in every room in every mirror. Don't let yourself question your gut. If you have a dream and you want it, you can have it, there is nothing stopping you from accomplishing anything. You are your best self and you are a person to be looked up to. Doubt is like the little devil sitting on your shoulder, the one we were taught not to listen to when we were children. Those little tales that we grew up with had a deeper meaning than we acknowledged. You are amazing. You have a goal. You set your goal. Don't worry about the middle part so much. If you want something deep enough and are willing to work hard enough in a very honest way, you can do it. Set doubt aside! There's no room for that in your life.

Gem #2 Negative energy and negative influence are two things that no one needs in their life.

Disregard everything that does not align with who you are. We all have choices in life. We choose our friends, we choose our hobbies and we choose to spend time with our family. If ever any of these choices or individuals have negative thoughts towards you and your goals or try to talk you out of them, say goodbye. Release yourself. As we get older we realize quality over quantity. There is love and forgiveness and forgiveness is so necessary in order to let go of the negative energy of the past. Let go of influences in your life that bring you down. You are strong. You have goals. You have YOU!

Gem #3 OPTIMISM

Be that person who sees the glass half full not the glass half empty. See the best of every situation. If you see a problem, try to find a solution and try to make that solution come from your heart. When you truly care about your clients or your neighbour or the lady in the grocery store line up that changes everything that comes your way. Optimism is something that is slowly being lost. People start losing faith in relationships, they start losing faith in faith, they have negative thoughts such as "maybe everything I have been planning has been a big mistake."

All of these little gems tie in together. Each one feeds the other and helps build strength and power and confidence.

I like many, am a person that was raised with a religious background. So for me, the Ten Commandments come into play a lot with balance. I think coming from strong moral beliefs has helped me become the person I am. I truly try to do onto others, as I would like done unto myself. But let's not try to fool anybody. Nobody's perfect. We all make mistakes but in doing this, you strive for personal perfection according to what your morals are. I'll never forget this one time I lay down in the dentist chair terrified (who likes the dentist chair?) but they had a poster on the ceiling and on that poster, I read, "Over tip your morning waitress and always be the first to say hello." This is just a tiny example of what I'm trying to get across. This little message has stuck with me throughout my entire life and I've always remembered to do both of these things. It's amazing how surprised people are when you just say hello. It brings joy and a smile to both of you!

About Nicole Stettler

Nicole Stettler is the Owner and lead esthetician of Optimal Esthetics Incorporated and Optimal Strength Rage Fitness, two downtown located business offering expertise in the overall wellness, esthetics, laser hair removal, as well as a boutique training facility for clients who seek one on one personal training and nutritional guidance for a healthier lifestyle.

Nicole was raised in a small town in interior BC. Coming from a family of entrepreneurs, she relocated to Calgary in her early twenties. She is now certified in IPL, Laser Hair Removal, basic and advanced skin anatomy, microdermabrasion, chemical peels, and advanced laser certification. She's also spent all of her life within the fitness industry. Certified as a Level one Crossfit Coach, Olympic Weightlifting, Crossfit Gymnastics, TRX, Zumba, International Sports Sciences Association Fitness Nutrition as well as ISSA Elite Personal Training Certification.

While Nicole is running her businesses she also cares for her two beautiful children. She has a passion to keep herself fit, with a love for skincare and a healthy fit lifestyle for herself and her children. She is a business owner, a fitness and face guru, and a devoted mother. Nicole believes in the lifestyle to pay it forward and tries to help all people around her.

I AM a brilliant woman as I try my best to do everything in life from my heart with the best intentions for my kids, myself and every living being that crosses into my world.

– Nicole Stettler

I AM a Brilliant Woman

About Women Embracing Brilliance

Women Embracing Brilliance was created to support, encourage and celebrate women who are committed to expressing their voice, reclaiming their feminine power and embracing the highest version of who they are – *their Brilliant Self.*

Our vision over the next five years is to positively impact the lives of women around the world by empowering them to embrace and stand in their boldness, brilliance, and beauty.

How? When one woman embraces her brilliance, her *soul signature* radiates out through her own voice of love, compassion, and encouragement, which plants a seed in those around her. That seed becomes a ripple effect igniting the light within others and contributing to the evolution of humanity.

We are a global community of heart-centered women who are dedicated to making a difference by empowering each other to live in optimal health, love, and prosperity. As we embrace and ignite our brilliance, we create heaven on earth for all.

Sign up and receive inspirational messages

that will help you to become your best self at karenklassen.ca

12516223R00077

Made in the USA
Monee, IL
26 September 2019